"Many come to seminary thinking that i [...] need to know for ministry, but seminar[y] [...] building. Some things are learned only th[...] [...] job training; which is to say, some things are learned only in life and in ministry. Hansen and Robinson have brought together a number of essays that convey the struggles and joys of pastoral ministry. They remind us that all successful pastoral ministry is a miracle, that apart from Jesus we can do nothing. Here we find words of wisdom that will help prepare future and present pastors for the road ahead."

Thomas R. Schreiner, James Buchanan Harrison Professor of New Testament Interpretation, The Southern Baptist Theological Seminary

"What would it be like if you could sit down with a dozen or so veteran pastors who have learned from their own successes and failures? What would you ask them, as an aspiring pastor or other church officer? This book is very helpful for all who realize that seminary can't teach them everything."

Michael Horton, J. Gresham Machen Professor of Theology and Apologetics, Westminster Seminary California; Host, *White Horse Inn*; author, *Core Christianity*

"In the few years of instruction it offers, a seminary cannot do everything. Often what is missing is getting oriented to the relational things that come with ministry, something a classroom does not teach us. Here is a book that tackles those other, mostly relational things. It does so with sensitivity and wisdom. I commend this book for the heart it can give to your ministry."

Darrell Bock, Executive Director of Cultural Engagement, The Hendricks Center, Dallas Theological Seminary

"We are blessed in our modern day to have some wonderful seminaries. And yet even the strongest seminaries fall short of equipping men with the practical tools every pastor needs in ministry. That is one of the many reasons this book is a brilliant, needed resource. *15 Things Seminary Couldn't Teach Me* is a gift not just for every seminary-trained pastor, but also for every man laboring in the trenches of pastoral ministry. An all-star cast of pastors has been assembled to fill this long-exposed gap in the training of pastors."

Brian Croft, Senior Pastor, Auburndale Baptist Church, Louisville, Kentucky; Founder, Practical Shepherding; Senior Fellow, Mathena Center for Church Revitalization, The Southern Baptist Theological Seminary

"I've come to realize that no matter how much seminary teaches us, there remain some massive lessons that no number of degrees can impart. Since the first step to learning is finding out what we do not know, open this book and begin a ministry-long educational journey in fifteen of the most important subjects of your life."

David Murray, Professor of Old Testament and Practical Theology, Puritan Reformed Theological Seminary

"Going to seminary is about more than picking up a few skills and getting an education. It is about getting a life. This book is about the contours of such a life, a life of ministry replete with swerves and curves, but sustained all the while by the grace of a God who calls and keeps. Every seminary student should read this book."

Timothy George, Founding Dean, Beeson Divinity School, Samford University; general editor, Reformation Commentary on Scripture

"I am grateful for the opportunities I have had to receive seminary training. Learning from men who have spent years thinking about biblical and theological matters can be invaluable. Tools and disciplines that I took away from my years of formal education have served me well. But no amount of seminary training can completely prepare a man for pastoral ministry. This book, by faithful men who have both years and scars in gospel ministry, is full of wisdom. Every pastor and aspiring pastor should read and benefit from their experience."

Tom Ascol, Executive Director, Founders Ministries; Pastor, Grace Baptist Church, Cape Coral, Florida

15 Things Seminary Couldn't Teach Me

Other Gospel Coalition Books

Coming Home: Essays on the New Heaven and New Earth, edited by D. A. Carson and Jeff Robinson Sr.

Don't Call It a Comeback: The Old Faith for a New Day, edited by Kevin DeYoung

Entrusted with the Gospel: Pastoral Expositions of 2 Timothy, edited by D. A. Carson

Glory in the Ordinary: Why Your Work in the Home Matters to God, by Courtney Reissig

God's Love Compels Us: Taking the Gospel to the World, edited by D. A. Carson and Kathleen B. Nielson

God's Word, Our Story: Learning from the Book of Nehemiah, edited by D. A. Carson and Kathleen B. Nielson

The Gospel as Center: Renewing Our Faith and Reforming Our Ministry Practices, edited by D. A. Carson and Timothy Keller

Gospel-Centered Youth Ministry: A Practical Guide, edited by Cameron Cole and Jon Nielson

Here Is Our God: God's Revelation of Himself in Scripture, edited by Kathleen B. Nielson and D. A. Carson

His Mission: Jesus in the Gospel of Luke, edited by D. A. Carson and Kathleen B. Nielson

The New City Catechism: 52 Questions and Answers for Our Hearts and Minds

The New City Catechism Devotional: God's Truth for Our Hearts and Minds

The Pastor as Scholar and the Scholar as Pastor: Reflections on Life and Ministry, by John Piper and D. A. Carson, edited by David Mathis and Owen Strachan

Praying Together: The Priority and Privilege of Prayer: In Our Homes, Communities, and Churches, by Megan Hill

Pursuing Health in an Anxious Age, by Bob Cutillo

The Scriptures Testify about Me: Jesus and the Gospel in the Old Testament, edited by D. A. Carson

Seasons of Waiting: Walking by Faith When Dreams Are Delayed, by Betsy Childs Howard

Word-Filled Women's Ministry: Loving and Serving the Church, edited by Gloria Furman and Kathleen B. Nielson

15 Things Seminary Couldn't Teach Me

Edited by
Collin Hansen and Jeff Robinson Sr.

Foreword by R. Albert Mohler Jr.

WHEATON, ILLINOIS

Trade paperback ISBN: 978-1-4335-5814-6
ePub ISBN: 978-1-4335-5817-7
PDF ISBN: 978-1-4335-5815-3
Mobipocket ISBN: 978-1-4335-5816-0

Library of Congress Cataloging-in-Publication Data

Names: Hansen, Collin, 1981– editor.
Title: 15 things seminary couldn't teach me / edited by Collin Hansen and Jeff Robinson Sr.; foreword by R. Albert Mohler.
Other titles: Fifteen things seminary couldn't teach me
Description: Wheaton: Crossway, 2018. | Series: The gospel coalition | Includes bibliographical references and index.
Identifiers: LCCN 2017022967 (print) | LCCN 2017059706 (ebook) | ISBN 9781433558153 (pdf) | ISBN 9781433558160 (mobi) | ISBN 9781433558177 (epub) | ISBN 9781433558146 (tp)
Subjects: LCSH: Pastoral theology.
Classification: LCC BV4011.3 (ebook) | LCC BV4011.3 .A13 2018 (print) | DDC 253/.2—dc23
LC record available at https://lccn.loc.gov/2017022967

Crossway is a publishing ministry of Good News Publishers.

VP		28	27	26	25	24	23	22	21	20	19	18
15	14	13	12	11	10	9	8	7	6	5	4	3	2	1

To Chris Castaldo,
who modeled the love of Jesus in his care
for me during the seminary years

Collin Hansen

———

To the faculty of
The Southern Baptist Theological Seminary,
who taught me by humble example
to be a pastor-theologian

Jeff Robinson Sr.

Contents

Foreword

You might think that a seminary president would be the last person to write the foreword to a book on what a seminary *didn't* provide for pastors. Actually, I welcome the opportunity. I have committed my life to the education of pastors through The Southern Baptist Theological Seminary, and after nearly twenty-five years of leading a seminary, I am more convinced than ever of the value of a seminary education.

But seminaries do not call pastors. God does. And seminaries do not make pastors. Churches do. Keeping that straight is important.

A good seminary can add immeasurably to a pastor's ministry, and the rigorous study involved in a quality seminary education should be expected of any preacher of the Word of God. The theological disciplines are of crucial importance, and though a faithful pastor will be more than a scholar, the church learned long ago the necessity of a learned ministry.

The most faithful seminary envisions itself as a servant of the churches, assisting the local church in the making of pastors. The seminary serves the church. The church does not serve the seminary. The paradigm for the education of a pastor in the New Testament is Timothy under the teaching and mentoring of the apostle Paul.

So we should not be surprised that experienced pastors would be able to detail and document the lessons of ministry that were not learned at seminary. In some cases, this may reflect poorly on the seminary, but in most cases it points profoundly to the centrality of the local church and to the lessons of ministry that can be learned only through ministry to a congregation.

The structure of a theological education has developed into a fairly standard pattern—three years of courses separated into biblical studies, theological studies, and ministry studies. There is a wealth of wisdom in that structure, which explains why almost every seminary finds its way into this pattern.

The weakest component has always been ministry studies. This is not due to a failure of the faculty, and most pastors look back on those courses as very helpful. So, what explains the weakness?

It is the important distinction between analysis and experience. I didn't identify the problem as theory as opposed to practice. Ministry studies in the seminary are not merely theoretical. But there is no teacher of ministry like the local church. The preacher should learn a great deal about preaching in the seminary but will become a true preacher only through the call and experience of preaching the Word to a congregation. In the best context, this means a senior pastor taking younger pastors under his care and teaching—the congregation invested fully in the perpetuation of a gospel ministry.

There are ample analogies. The United States Military Academy at West Point exists for good reason, but officers are made by leading troops and fighting battles. I would not want to have surgery at the hands of a physician who had not graduated (with high honors) from a good medical school. But I'd also want to know that the surgeon had trained with the very best doctors in residency and had performed the procedure many times.

You get the point.

I would actually be interested in reading a book of essays by veteran army generals on what they did not learn at West Point. It might be that West Point would gain some important information from such a book and take it to heart. My guess is that most of those essays would look back to West Point with deep appreciation and affection, while understanding that some lessons have always been learned only in the crucible of war. I'll also bet that those generals would be incredibly glad they did not go to battle without that West Point education.

And so it is with the Christian ministry. The essays in this book, seasoned with thoughtfulness and seeded with experience, are really helpful in clarifying the centrality of the local church in the education of a pastor. Some of the essays will make you smile; others may make you wince. Every essay will make you think.

This book will be helpful to new pastors, pastors of long tenure, seminary leaders and professors, and seminary students. Up front, these essays will help seminary students to prepare for ministry. Then, given enough experience in ministry, the thoughtful pastor would be able to contribute on his own not only an essay like one of these, but an entire book of essays.

The faithful pastor needs an education in exegesis but is made in the preparation and delivery of sermons to the people of God. That pastor needs the theological studies gained in seminary, but that theology is eventually hammered out when the pastor is called to preach the funeral of a child. A background in hermeneutics and homiletics is vital, but the preacher discovers his real method of interpretation and his real understanding of preaching when deciding how to preach a specific text to a specific people—and then preaching to the same congregation again and again and again.

I would read the *What West Point Couldn't Teach Me* book with genuine interest. You will read this book with nothing less than urgency. Don't miss a single lesson to be learned—but keep in mind that every pastor learns the most important lessons only through years of ministry. At the same time, learn as much as you can before you hit the battlefield alone. It matters.

R. Albert Mohler Jr.

1

Knowledge and Credentials Aren't Enough

Jeff Robinson Sr.

I warned them, but I don't think they believed me.

No doubt, they thought I was merely trying to exhibit humility or was trafficking in a garden-variety form of preacher talk. The pastoral search committee had zeroed in on me as its final candidate, but the three letters that sometimes appear to the right of my name kept hijacking our conversation: PhD.

"Should we call you doctor?" one asked. "I'll bet you'll really get this church going with all you bring to the table as a doctor," another said. I fidgeted in my seat. I didn't doubt the sincerity of their admiration, but I felt profoundly unprepared to play the role of spiritual superhero.

I had no idea.

At last, I said: "I'm grateful you want to honor my studies, but please don't mistake a degree for maturity, fitness for ministry, or competence, and certainly not for godliness. The one does not necessarily portend the others. All it really means is that I persevered long enough to meet some academic requirements."

From the standpoint of interview skill, that was the correct answer. But over the next three years, God burned the truth of those words deep into the recesses of my soul.

Soon, the church called me as senior pastor. Soon, I learned that advanced degrees from a leading theological institution had not transformed me into the godly, humble, wise, selfless leader this congregation desperately needed. Soon, I realized only suffering-laden service on the front lines of ministry could make me that man. Soon, it hit me: I serve the church at war.

Sadly, my tenure in that first pastorate lasted little more than three years, due mostly to a major financial crisis in the church. Today, I am privileged to serve a different congregation. And thanks to lessons learned from many mistakes and foolhardy decisions I made in the first church, I am a different pastor. My prayer is that the good people in my current field of service will benefit from the hard lessons learned in the earlier work.

I also serve as an adjunct professor at the seminary that trained me, so I am deeply invested in the lives of future pastors. I have a love for the church and for theological education that serves the church, but the pastoral ministry has taught me three major lessons that I could have learned only by serving God's people in the local church, and those lessons form the basis and the rationale for the book you are now reading: credentials are not competence, ministry means war, and apart from God's absolute, unilateral grace, a pastor labors in vain.

Credentials Are Not Competence

Prior to becoming a pastor, I had preached 1 Corinthians 13 many times and had seen it cross-stitched on home decor at least a thousand more. But once I began to shepherd a local flock, Paul's words became one of the most perplexing passages to me in the entire Bible. Why? It's not difficult to interpret, but therein lies the rub; it's difficult because it's easier to be orthodox than it is to be loving.

And knowledge puffs up. As one who prizes the study of theology and church history, that phrase hits close to home. It hits home because, if God gave me one wish in a prosperity-theology sort of way, I'd be tempted to choose "have all knowledge" instead of "be perfect in holiness."

Every hour of seminary delighted my soul. It left me with much knowledge, and, as it is designed to do, equipped me to gain more for myself. But I soon realized that my command of Greek or Hebrew or the Puritans is not enough to keep me from erupting when an angry church member brings false charges against me. Those things don't necessarily provide wise leadership decisions when a deacon tells me that the church is almost out of money.

Sure, my theological knowledge positions me to make wise decisions and enables me to feed the flock with healthy grass, but the maturity needed to be a godly under-shepherd comes only through days, weeks, months, and years of labor in the vineyard of the Lord. It didn't take long for me to realize that I am a man in the middle of his sanctification, just like the people who listen to me preach every Lord's day.

Love Surpasses Knowledge

Soon, I realized the people under my care were not all that interested in my orthodoxy, although I could never compromise it. They really wanted to know if I loved them. Once they knew that I genuinely cared and saw them as cherished family in Christ—and not so much as subjects for evangelism or discipleship—they were much more willing to listen to my attempts at expounding orthodoxy.

There was only one means for building such a relationship: time in their presence.

I recall one particularly cranky man who just didn't seem to like me—at first. So, taking a page from the Richard Baxter playbook, I visited his home. It was summer and we sat on his porch. We talked about the respective football teams at Auburn and my alma mater, Georgia. I listened to him talk about Dale Earnhardt. I listened to his wife talk about her family's role in the founding of our church.

Before long, they seemed to move into my corner. On the day I left the church, he bear-hugged me and, through a river of tears, told me how his family had grown to love mine and how they would miss us. They would miss my teaching, too, he said.

Love never fails, and love surpasses knowledge.

The inspired writer warned me about this: "If I have . . . all knowledge . . . but have not love, I am nothing" (1 Cor. 13:2). If I do not love my people, they will not care how much theological talk comes from the pulpit. They will follow me only when I prove that I love them and can be trusted as a mature teacher and under-shepherd.

In his excellent book *Dangerous Calling: Confronting the Unique Challenges of Pastoral Ministry*, Paul David Tripp, a longtime pastor and seminary professor, identifies a binary syndrome that too often inflicts the inexperienced but self-assured pastor. Tripp appropriately labels this dangerous malady as "big theological brains and heart disease":

> Bad things happen when maturity is more defined by knowing than it is by being. Danger is afloat when you come to love ideas more than the God whom they represent and the people they are meant to free.
>
> . . . I longed for [seminary students] to understand that they aren't called just to *teach* theology to their people but also to *do* theology with their people.[1]

The apostle, after reciting his lengthy biological, theological, and experiential pedigree, concluded much the same: "I have reason for confidence in the flesh, but whatever gain I had, I have counted loss for the sake of Christ" (Phil. 3:8). From a worldly standpoint, Paul possessed all the ingredients to serve as an omni-competent pastor, yet it was all rubbish compared with knowing Christ and exhibiting his love for people.

If you have served in a local church for long, a second lesson will

---

1. Paul David Tripp, *Dangerous Calling: Confronting the Unique Challenges of Pastoral Ministry* (Wheaton, IL: Crossway, 2012), 42–43.

become axiomatic for you: ministry means war, which is to say, suffering is the norm for God's under-shepherd, but it is good.

Ministry Means War

A. W. Tozer famously said, "It is doubtful whether God can bless a man greatly until He has hurt him deeply."[2] In the ministry, as in the Christian life, there is no crown without a cross. The great men of Scripture were formed under the lash of suffering—Job, Daniel, King David, Peter, Paul, and, of course, our Lord Jesus Christ.

The great names in church history walked the Calvary road of affliction. Luther and Calvin were forced to run for their lives. John Bunyan spent twelve years in a Bedford jail for preaching the gospel. Charles Simeon served an irascible congregation that once locked him out of the church. I had a friend whose church fired him because he planted grass at the parsonage without a committee's permission. Another friend was sent away two weeks after being elected because a deacon found an objectionable theology book in his library as the moving van was being unloaded.

How bad can it get? The cauldron of suffering nearly drove the great Charles Spurgeon from the ministry at the age of twenty-two. On October 19, 1856, seven people were killed and twenty-eight injured when someone shouted "Fire!" during a Sunday evening service at the Surrey Garden Music Hall, causing hundreds of the twelve thousand gathered to stampede.

The depression that resulted from this disaster left Spurgeon prostrate for days. "Even the sight of the Bible, brought from me a flood of tears, and utter distraction of mind."[3] This set the tone for his ministry, and he battled acute anxiety and dark depression the rest of his life.

Seminary did not teach me how deeply ministry could wound. But it *couldn't* teach me that, for seminary is to ministry what basic training is to combat: a training ground, a relatively safe place to

---

2. A. W. Tozer, *The Root of the Righteous* (Chicago: Moody Publishers, 2015), 165; originally published 1955.

3. *The Autobiography of Charles H. Spurgeon*, compiled by his wife and his private secretary, vol. 2 (New York: Revell, 1899), 207.

acquire the tools of ministry—Greek, Hebrew, exegesis, homiletics, systematic theology, church history, and much more. Basic training is not war, and seminary is not local church ministry. Nothing but the battlefield of ministry could have prepared me for the pain ahead.

Yet, had I been paying closer attention to Scripture, I would have seen the warning signs. Through the lens of Paul's ministry, 2 Corinthians is a manual for suffering in pastoral ministry. Read a few verses and you'll see the office of elder is not for the faint of heart. It is dangerous, even deadly. It will bruise the new man I'm becoming in Christ, and it will kill the old man I was before the grace of God stormed the battlements of my heart. It is a glorious death sentence from the hand of a loving God. In 2 Corinthians 11:23–28, Paul contrasts his ministry with that of the so-called "super-apostles" (2 Cor. 11:5). The apostle offers his own ministry résumé. It includes such items as five times receiving forty lashes less one, being beaten with rods three times, being shipwrecked three times, sleeplessness, hunger, thirst, and danger. Tough stuff. And Paul is mostly describing the war that rages outside the pastor. Perhaps a more intense and potentially bloody battle plays out in another theater—the heart of the pastor.

The War Within

There will be difficult days in ministry. You will doubt your calling. You will question God's goodness. Your heart will struggle to trust the divine sovereignty your mouth has so often celebrated. You will fear people. You will resent the apparent ministry success of your friends, though pride will lead you to publicly congratulate them. You will want to quit, particularly on Mondays. To summarize: you will wrestle with you.

Voices will fill your ears with an alluring siren song, urging you to find, by whatever means necessary—even by small increments of theological or ethical compromise—a place where ease and earthly prosperity reign. There, in ministerial Rivendell, you will be far from the bad deacons meeting, far from the church member whose marriage is imploding, far from the family who thinks you are killing the church by teaching the Bible instead of building the youth group.

This is the internal battle of Ephesians 6:17, and it is intensified within the minister because of his calling. If you are to survive this war, you must feed upon God's Word daily. You must become a man of constant prayer, of vigilant self-examination. You must live in habitual awareness that you utterly depend upon the grace of God. Paul asked the question in 1 Corinthians 4:7 to which you must learn the correct answer: "What do you have that you did not receive?" Absolutely nothing.

Suffering is normal in ministry. Paul suffered. Our heroes from church history suffered. Affliction is at the heart of the gospel as our Lord suffered in our place. God will use this struggle with foes from without and within to make us more like Jesus, to slay our pride, to arm us with gospel comfort so we may comfort fellow sufferers in our charge, and, perhaps above all, to provide the church with a picture of the sufferings of Christ. Humiliation precedes exaltation, both for Christ and for his people (2 Cor. 4:7–12). It's the gospel way.

Affliction will either drive God's servants to my third and final lesson or drive them from ministry.

Apart from Him You Can Do Nothing

One phrase the minister must burn above the doorpost of his heart is our Lord's words in John 15:5: "Apart from me you can do nothing." If you are to persevere in faithfulness, God's undiluted, unilateral grace must uphold you. Various studies communicate a grim but unified message: a high percentage of seminary graduates disappear permanently from gospel ministry within five years. You will need grace upon grace upon grace.

In the context of his being lifted up to the third heaven in 2 Corinthians 12, the apostle tells his readers that God does not weigh strength on the same scales as we do: "I will boast all the more gladly of my weaknesses, so that the power of Christ may rest upon me. . . . For when I am weak, then I am strong" (12:9–10). Paul realizes that only the grace of God makes his ministry effective. Paul has no strength in himself—only that which the Lord gives him.

He Alone Makes Dry Bones Live

A few days into that first pastorate, I realized that only the Lord working through his Word and his Spirit could make dry bones live. All I could do was preach the Word, pray, and shepherd God's sheep. Mercifully, the pressure is not on us to change hearts. The gospel is the power of God for salvation. In 2 Corinthians 4:7–12, Paul aptly summarized the minister's place in the economy of God's work: "But we have this treasure in jars of clay, to show that the surpassing power belongs to God and not to us" (4:7).

That's good news! The power belongs to God. I don't have to muster it—I cannot muster it. God takes his preached Word and transforms sinful people. Faith comes by hearing, and hearing through the Word of Christ (Rom. 10:17). We sow the seed. God grows the seed. God's ministers—as God's people—utterly depend upon him.

Conclusion

At Kings Island amusement park near Cincinnati, there was once a wooden roller coaster that stood more than three hundred feet tall. At the entrance, there was a sign that said, "This ride is not for the faint of heart." Pastoral ministry is like that. It is a delightful calling with many dizzying highs. It is a dangerous calling with many depressing lows. It will rattle your bones all along the way.

But preaching God's Word and watching him use it to transform lives is a marvel that strains the descriptive capacity of human words. Yet Paul's words reflect my assessment of the ministry God has given me: "Woe to me if I do not preach the gospel!" (1 Cor. 9:16).

2

What to Do When My Church Is Dying

Mark Vroegop

"We have to love our people more than we hate where they're at."

I said this in a staff meeting as my fellow pastors and I wrestled with yet another frustrating issue within our congregation. I often quoted this line as a mantra for them and myself as we struggled to help our hurting church. A few years earlier, after serving as associate pastor, I accepted the call to be senior pastor, not fully understanding the challenges I would encounter.

Don't get me wrong; I knew there would be issues. But this particular church came from a challenging church tradition. When friends asked about the church's background, I would say, "Independent, fundamentalist, King-James-only, Beulah-Land-singing kind of church."

Enough said.

And there was more: The church had never practiced church discipline, despite multiple moral failures from some of its people. And, as I learned, the church did not have a great reputation in the community, being mostly known for what it was against and not what it was for. The church building was adequate, the budget stable, and attendance steady. But the church was slowly dying—more than any of us probably knew.

Over the next decade, I set out on a mission to help the church become healthy again. It wasn't easy. I made some mistakes. It took a lot of patience, tears, and prayer. However, the journey was worth it because of what God did in the life of that church, and what he did in me.

Ten Years, Seven Lessons

With another ten years in the mirror since that season, and while now serving in another church ministry, I can see now how to help a dying church, and it boils down to seven key elements.

1. Love Them

The primacy of love in pastoral ministry cannot be overstated. According to 1 Corinthians 13, without love, nothing else matters. It is foundational. Love, as defined in this passage—being patient and kind, not envying or being boastful, not being proud or rude, not insisting on your own way, not being irritable or resentful, and not rejoicing in wrongdoing—applies as much to pastoral leadership as to marriage or other relationships.

You can't help people without loving them, and a congregation needs to know that its pastor loves and understands the church. It is hard to trust and follow someone who doesn't know you or who seems angry with you, especially in something as personal as church ministry.

A major reason I accepted the call to a church I knew would be difficult was that I already loved the people as their associate pastor. I knew their stories and history. I heard about their disappointments and struggles. And I longed for a better day for them. I wanted to be a part of their future because they had gotten into my heart.

Bearing all things, believing all things, hoping all things, and enduring all things—that's where we have to start.

2. Faithfully Teach the Bible

Another key lesson relates to the effect of faithfully teaching people the Bible week after week. I knew my main task was to preach and teach Scripture faithfully and expositionally, but I didn't realize how effective a weekly verse-by-verse approach would be in restoring health to the body.

For example, as I was teaching through Matthew 18, I helped the congregation see the need to practice church discipline. As I taught through Ephesians 4, we talked about what it means for pastors to equip the church for the work of the ministry. As I taught through Galatians, we identified the dangers of legalism. Week after week our people learned what the Bible said and how it applied to our church. There was no single Sunday where everything changed, but every Sunday *something* changed. It was slow and sometimes invisible, but over time, the church became healthier as we learned together how to think and live biblically.

3. Take the Long View

Pastoral patience is underrated these days. From every angle we are bombarded with quick fixes, fast changes, and a desire for immediate results. I know many pastors who are thinking in months when they should thinking years or maybe even decades. Being patient is not usually a top-tier, celebrated characteristic of pastors. But it should be.

Much like parenting, spiritual growth and congregational renewal take time—a long time. There are a thousand consistent actions you hope and pray will yield fruit over the long haul. Old thinking patterns, habits, and traditions do not change easily; truth has to be applied multiple times in multiple ways before it becomes familiar and accepted. And people need time to see what health looks like. They didn't get where they are overnight, and many changes take time.

Faithful, patient, consistent, and persevering leadership that thinks in decades instead of weeks is key. To help a dying church, take the long view.

4. *Trust in God's Providence*

Giving help to a struggling church requires confidence in God's providential care for the congregation and for you. My wife and I knew God had called us into ministry, and we also knew he called us to this particular church. We had wrestled with God's will, walked through the candidate process, and clearly sensed God's call to shepherd this church. Knowing our assignment was from the Lord provided a firm anchor for our souls when things were difficult, painful, or frustrating. I remember driving home from a discouraging meeting and crying out to the Lord: "Why did you send me here!" The silence from heaven eventually gave way to a personal reminder that it was indeed the Lord who called us. The way forward just wasn't yet clear. I needed to keep trusting. If God called us, he would help us. And he did.

But trust must go even further. Every church belongs to God. It is his bride, and God is the one orchestrating its story. To effectively lead a church to health, a pastor must live out his belief in God's providence as controversies emerge, people leave, new people come, finances change, people are converted, cultural pressures emerge, and sin is revealed. There was a particular season when it seemed as if secret sins were coming to light with unusual frequency. One morning, exhausted and discouraged, I read this statement from a devotional by D. A. Carson about the exposure of Ananias and Sapphira's sin in Acts 5: "When God walks away from the church and lets the multiplying sin take its course, that is the worst judgment of all; it will inevitably end in irretrievable disaster. But when God responds to sin with prompt severity, lessons are learned, and the church is spared a worse drift."[1] Once again, the Lord reminded me to trust him.

---

1. D. A. Carson, "July 18," in *For the Love of God: A Daily Companion for Discovering the Riches of God's Word*, vol. 1 (Wheaton, IL: Crossway, 1998).

Helping a church change requires a deep commitment to live out your theology of God's providential care for you and the church.

5. Look in the Mirror

In the course of helping a church change, both the pastor and the church may need to take a careful look in the mirror to see what changes will restore life.

Sometimes a church can be stuck in the past, using outdated and ineffective ministry forms. Perhaps the church's culture is inhospitable to visitors, or the reputation of the church is poor in the community. There may be unhealthy leadership teams or staff members who are not on board with changes. Any of these can be a recipe for an unhealthy ministry, and a wise pastor will carefully and honestly evaluate if internal issues and ineffective strategies are causing the church to lose spiritual momentum.

But the church is not alone in needing a mirror. Pastors need one too, and here's where a few helpful and loving people can be a major asset. Every person in ministry has blind spots, and sometimes those areas cause unintentional spiritual decline. For example, after about two years of preaching, my sermons became longer and longer. What started as forty-minute sermons soon became fifty and then sixty minutes long. I loved what I was learning and wanted to share it all. But I was wearing my people out—even frustrating them as the services consistently dragged on and on. Finally, a loving brother pointed this out and encouraged me to share only what was truly important. Without his courage and kindness, who knows how long my sermons would have become?

6. Think Like a Missionary

Not many pastors think like missionaries when it comes to their churches. They assume that all churches made up of people who speak the same language, live in the same country, or have the same evangelical theology are basically the same. But it's rarely that simple, and to think it is misses the critical issue of cultural contextualization.

Every church and every member has a story, a history, a culture, and a worldview. And a wise pastor will work hard to research and understand that culture. To help a church change, you must exegete the church's context.

In my challenging situation, I treated the church as a people group I was trying to reach. I met with individuals to learn each one's story. I asked lots of questions and looked for patterns, themes, or defining moments. I gently dug into previous controversies and learned what did or didn't happen. I read what my people were reading, visited them at their workplaces, prayed with them in the hospital, and listened to their painful memories when loved ones passed. I wanted to understand them. And I wanted them to know I understood.

That research never stopped. I kept learning not only because new questions emerged, but also because I saw the benefit of becoming a student of my people. It helped me preach more effectively and allowed me to know which issues would need more time.

A fellow pastor and I met for lunch because he was in the midst of a significant church conflict. He needed help. The issue centered on his decision to remove the American and Christian flags from the platform. I winced at his story. He had been the pastor for only a few years, and I knew his church was filled with an unusual number of veterans. While I agreed with his decision in theory, I could see how needlessly controversial this issue was. Had he taken enough time to exegete his people and listen to their stories, he would have learned that the flag issue was larger than first appeared. He would have known how and when to address it.

In failing to think like a missionary, he violated the trust of his people. Unfortunately, that was not the only violation. He tried to change things too quickly and unwisely, and a few months later he and the church parted ways.

Missionaries are not the only ministry leaders who need to think carefully about contextual issues such as the setting, tradition, history, and symbols of a particular group of people. Every church has a story and a culture. Helping churches change requires thinking like a missionary.

7. Pray, Pray, Pray

Finally, helping a struggling church requires a faithful commitment to prayer. Without this essential component of personal and pastoral ministry, changing a church can be an exercise in self-will. A friend of mine says, "Prayerlessness is our declaration of independency from God." Pastors must stay utterly dependent on God to lead the people; therefore, it is critical to pray for your people. I found praying for people by name helped fan the flames of love for them. I saw God answer prayers as people began to grow and change. I saw God answer prayers for new people, and I saw him lead people elsewhere who were not supportive of our direction.

My prayer journals were spiritual ballast for my soul.

Pastors also need to pray *with* their people. My first church, for all its weaknesses, knew how to pray. Every Saturday morning for nearly eight years I met with a group of men to pray for our church. Listening to their prayers taught me how to pray more effectively, and it knit my heart to these men as we brought the church's needs before the Lord.

Our prayer time became a weekly reset for my soul and pastoral heart. God alone knows how our faithful devotion to seeking him about our members, our future, and our hearts played a part in the church's growth and health, but I know it shaped my heart as their pastor.

I Really Feel Loved Today

How do you help a struggling or dying church? No one taught me how to do that in seminary, despite the many churches that need to change. What those hurting churches need are wise, loving, patient, prayerful, and thoughtful shepherds to lead them to new life and health.

A number of years into my pastorate, I decided it was time for me to change the Bible translation I used in preaching. Years earlier this issue would have been divisive, but over time most of the people no longer thought it was an issue. However, there were still four families for whom it might have been offensive. A few months before I made the switch I met with each family and shared with them what I was going to do and why. I wanted them to hear not only my rationale but also my heart for them, knowing they might not agree.

Their responses affirmed the church was making progress. Each family, even if they were not completely supportive, expressed gratitude for the conversation. One member said, "Pastor, I would have really opposed this a few years ago, but I trust you. It's not my preference, but that's okay." Another member said, "Thanks for talking this through with me. I really feel loved today."

In just a few years an issue that would have divided the church and created another painful controversy not only was well received but also became an opportunity to demonstrate love and compassion for the church. This strategy worked in other areas as well, allowing more change and growth to take place over time. What's more, it led the church to long-term health. Today and under the leadership of another pastor, the church is healthy and thriving.

Helping a church change is not for the faint of heart. It is for those who will love their people more than they hate where they're at.

3

How to Shepherd My Wife

Daniel L. Akin

My wife, Charlotte, and I got married young. She was nineteen and I was twenty-one. I came from a good Christian home. My parents and grandparents were all Christians. Charlotte, in stark contrast, came out of a broken home. Both of her parents were alcoholics. They divorced when she was seven. At age nine she, her sister, and her brother were placed in the Georgia Baptist Children's Home, where she lived until she was eighteen. During those years she almost never saw her parents. Her father did not attend our wedding, though he lived in the Atlanta area where we were married.

I say all this to point out that we came into our marriage with very different perspectives and expectations. I knew what a good home was and recognized that good was good. Perfection, though the ideal, would not be reached in this life since marriage is two sinners (saved by grace if they know Jesus!) living in close proximity.

Charlotte was absolutely determined not to follow in the footsteps of her parents. She was going to have the perfect marriage if it killed us both (and it nearly did on more than a few occasions)!

Add to this that we had no premarital counseling, for three reasons: (1) The year before we married, I attended Bible college in Dallas, and she was in Atlanta living with my parents. (2) The week before we married, our pastor—who married us—announced that he and his wife were getting a divorce. The one time we did meet with him, he apologized through tears, saying he really did not feel he could say anything to us. (3) In almost seven years of Bible college and seminary, I had exactly one class on marriage and family, which came outside my seminary education. I have no memory of a discussion on the home in seminary. None at all.

Given this background, you can imagine that our early days of marriage were quite challenging. Some were downright trying. Charlotte and I loved each other, and divorce was never an option, but all was not blissful, and the sailing was not smooth. We had some tough days.

I am writing this piece having just celebrated our thirty-eighth wedding anniversary. I can honestly say that outside of Jesus, nothing has brought me more happiness and joy than being a husband, father, and grandfather. But it has been hard work, and no one in seminary ever told me it would be. I have learned through the years and in the school of "hard knocks" that there are things I could have done to shepherd my wife more effectively and lovingly. Unfortunately, I didn't learn these things during my years in seminary.

Unwitting Marriage Counselor

I did learn about shepherding my wife by doing expository preaching—by walking verse by verse through Ephesians, in particular, and coming to 5:25–33. From this classic text on what it means to be a Spirit-filled (don't miss the prior context of 5:15–21, especially v. 18), Christlike husband, I learned five truths that every husband should plant deep in his heart as he strives to care well for the gift from God that is his wife. From these I will then make some specific applications.

1. Love Your Wife Sacrificially (Eph. 5:25)

The Bible tells husbands, "Love your wives, as Christ loved the church and gave himself up for her." "Love" here is a command. This tips us off to an important insight. Though love often has an emotional component, it is more of a volitional choice or decision. I choose, as an act of will, to love my wife whether I feel like it or not. It is not, "I love her if she . . . " It is not, "I love her because she . . . " No, it is, "I love her. Period." I love her even when she is not acting lovely, because that is exactly how Jesus loved me when he died on the cross, bore the wrath of God, and paid in full the penalty for all my sins. I was not lovely. He loved me in spite of me. He loved me unconditionally. He loved me and sacrificed himself in my place.

Husbands, it is one thing to love your wife sacrificially in the big things (e.g., I would die for her!). Will you, however, die daily for her in the small things? True sacrificial love aspires and works hard to do both.

2. Love Her Sanctifyingly (Eph. 5:26–27)

Verses 26–27 speak of a love that cleanses and washes, a love that makes something splendid, without blemish or wrinkle, holy and blameless. These verses used to confuse me when it came to my marriage. I mean, it is easy to see how this works for Christ and the church. He redeems us, he sanctifies us, and someday he will glorify us. Great! So what is the marriage connection? I believe it is something like this: because Charlotte is married to me, she is encouraged and enabled to grow to be more like Jesus. Ouch! That hurts. *Because* she is married to me—not *in spite of* being married to me—she is growing in her sanctification. She is growing in Christlikeness. I find this deeply convicting. Why? Because often I am not helping her become more like Jesus. I am more of a hindrance through neglect, impatience, a short fuse, and a busy schedule.

When we do new student orientation at Southeastern Seminary, I always encourage the incoming students to block off quality time for their wives and children. I plead with them to not let seminary or ministry become a mistress. Don't misunderstand me. Faithful

ministry requires hard work—a major investment of time and sacrifice. But you must not sacrifice your marriage on the humanly con-
trived altar of an idol. The sanctification of a minister's wife is built
into his God-given job description. If a pastor is going to disciple
anyone, it should start with his mate and his children.

3. Love Her Sensitively (Eph. 5:28–30)

Paul tells husbands that they are to "love their wives as their own
bodies. He who loves his wife loves himself" (5:28). He then gives
the rationale for this admonition: "For no one ever hated his own
flesh, but nourishes and cherishes it, just as Christ does the church"
(5:29). Paul's point is this: Husbands, you take care of yourself. You
know when you're having a good day and when you're having a bad
day. You know when things are up and when things are down. In the
same way, you should be sensitive to the needs of your wife.

I like to use the image of a "marital radar system." I am sending out
signals to my wife, and I am receiving signals back. I must confess that
early in my marriage, though I had all of the marital radar equipment
given me by God, it was in desperate need of construction and refine-
ment. At the thirty-eight-year mark of marriage, I must also confess
that I have not reached the end of my journey. But I do think Charlotte
would say I'm much more sensitive to her needs as a woman than I
was almost forty years ago. To love your wife in a sensitive way, you
have to spend time with her. Indeed, you must become a student of
your wife. Brothers, recognize that this is a school you will be in for
the rest of your life!

4. Love Her Satisfyingly (Eph. 5:31–32)

Not surprisingly Paul grounds his theology of marriage in two
places: (1) the cross work of Christ and (2) the order of creation
prior to the fall. In verse 31 he cites Genesis 2:24: "Therefore a man
shall leave his father and his mother and hold fast to his wife, and
they shall become one flesh." He goes on to affirm that this is a mystery when it comes to Christ and the church. I believe, by implica-
tion, that he would say it is a mystery when it comes to a man and a

woman as well. However, this leaving and cleaving, this going and joining, brings satisfaction to the heart of a wife.

It affirms the value you see in her, and it communicates that she has now become one with you. She is now your primary concern and focus of attention. I gladly confess that outside of the intimacy I enjoy personally with my Lord Jesus Christ, there is no intimacy, no satisfaction, like that which is shared in the wonderful covenant of marriage. Finding satisfaction in the wife of one's youth is indeed a good gift from a great God.

5. Love Her Specifically (Eph. 5:33)

Paul brings to a close his instruction to men by saying, "Let each one of you love his wife as himself." To restate this simply, Paul is calling every husband to be "a one-woman kind of man." This means that when it comes to my example as a husband, my friends know, my family knows, even my enemies know, that Danny Akin is a one-woman kind of man. He is in love with, devoted to, and committed to only one woman on this planet, and her name is Charlotte.

I'm often reminded and even warned by the tragic story of a man who was after God's own heart. We know this man to be King David. From his tragic story, I want to introduce a little formula that has guided me now almost four decades. I pass this on to you with the hope that it will provide good counsel and protection in your life as well. The formula: "The wrong person + the wrong place + the wrong time = the wrong thing happening."

King David, the man after God's own heart, was in the wrong place at the wrong time and with the wrong person. The results? He lied, he committed adultery, he murdered. If something like this could happen to a man after God's own heart, it could certainly happen to someone with Danny Akin's heart. Let people accuse you of being sexist. Let them even accuse you of being a scaredy-cat! But if you go to your grave having been faithful to your marital covenant, you'll have the smile of heaven as well as the smile of your wife.

Let me now turn to some practical applications. I have had the joy of doing marriage and family conferences for several decades.

You could say it is my spiritual hobby. Charlotte says I need to do at least one a month because I keep forgetting what I teach! Unfortunately, there is quite a bit of truth in those words.

When it comes to husbands, I first do an exposition of Ephesians 5:25–33. Then, I build on that foundation, draw from other relevant passages, and share seven practical ways to bless your wife day in and day out. I would argue that these ideas are true for every husband. I would also argue that they are especially needful for those who shepherd God's flock. I wish I had been taught these things in seminary. But better later than never.

Seven Ways to Bless Your Wife

A husband can be a blessing to his wife by loving her as Christ loved the church and giving her specific gifts of love. Here are seven:

1. *Be a spiritual leader.* Be a man of godly courage, conviction, commitment, compassion, and character. Take the initiative in cultivating a spiritual environment for your family. Become a capable and competent student of Scripture, and live all of life on the basis of God's Word. Nurture your wife in her growth as a woman of God, and take the lead in training your children in the things of the Lord (Psalm 1; Eph. 5:23–27).

2. *Give your wife personal affirmation and appreciation.* Praise her personal attributes and qualities. Speak of her virtues as a wife, mother, and homemaker. Openly commend her in the hearing of others as a marvelous mate, friend, lover, and companion. Help her feel that no one in this world is more important to you (Prov. 31:28–29; Song 4:1–7; 6:4–9; 7:1–9).

3. *Show personal affection (romance).* Shower her with timely and generous displays of affection. Tell her how much you care for her with a steady flow of words, cards, flowers, gifts, and common courtesies. Remember, affection is the environment in which sexual union is enjoyed more fully and a wonderful marriage is developed (Song 6:10, 13; Eph. 5:28–29, 33).

4. *Initiate intimate conversation.* Talk with her at the level of feelings (heart to heart). Listen to her thoughts (her heart) about

the events of her day with sensitivity, interest, and concern. Let your conversations with her convey a desire to understand her—not to change her (Song 2:8–14; 8:13–14; 1 Pet. 3:7). Changing her is God's job, not yours.

5. *Always be honest and open.* Look into her eyes and, in love, always tell her the truth (Eph. 4:15). Explain your plans and actions clearly and completely because you are responsible for her. Lead her to trust you and feel secure (Prov. 15:22–23).

6. *Provide home support and stability.* Shoulder the responsibility to house, feed, and clothe your family. Provide and protect, and resist feeling sorry for yourself when things get tough. Look for concrete ways to improve home life. Raise your marriage and family to a safer and more fulfilling level. Remember, the husband and father is the security hub of the family (1 Tim. 5:8).

7. *Demonstrate family commitment.* After the Lord Jesus, put your wife and family first. Commit time and energy to spiritual, moral, and intellectual development of your children. For example, pray with them (especially at night at bedside), read to them, engage in sports with them, and take them on other outings. Do not play the fool's game of working long hours, trying to get ahead, while your spouse and children languish in neglect (Eph. 6:4; Col. 3:19–20).[1]

Taught by the Word

These are things I did not learn in seminary. I had to learn them in life. And I'm grateful I learned them from expositing the Word of God!

---

1. For related discussion, see also Daniel L. Akin, "Pastor as Husband and Father," in *Portraits of a Pastor: The 9 Essential Roles of a Church Leader*, ed. Jason K. Allen (Chicago: Moody Publishers, 2017), and Akin, *Exalting Jesus in Song of Songs* (Nashville: B&H, 2015).

4

How to Pastor People Who Are Different from Me

Jeff Higbie

I had only ever lived in large suburbs of major metropolitan cities (Los Angeles; Washington, DC; and Chicago). So it made sense that God would call me to pastor a rural church right out of seminary. The population of Underwood, North Dakota, is less than a thousand, and the entire county is little more than ten thousand.

The church I had been part of for the previous decade in Evanston, Illinois, consisted largely of twenty- to thirty-somethings. When my wife and I first came to Faith Evangelical Church in 2007, I joked with our family and friends—though it was true at the time—that we were the youngest people in the congregation who were not still in school or living at home.

I enjoy going to the movies and watching professional sports. But the main pastimes in our area include hunting and fishing. The closest multiplex movie theater is fifty miles away, and the closest major league team, in any sport, is in Minneapolis (eight hours away!).

But having served in a rural, older, and outdoorsy community now for more than eight years, I can honestly say I have come to appreciate pastoring people who are different from me, and God has blessed and grown both me and also those I have been called to pastor.

So my goal is to spare you from reinventing the wheel, so you can begin on the right foot wherever God calls you, even if it is different from your background. I also want to help you be open to God calling you to shepherd those whose cultural, demographic, and theological backgrounds may be quite different from your own.

One book I highly recommend that every future pastor read before his first pastorate, and reread before starting at a new church, is *The Deliberate Church: Building Your Ministry on the Gospel*, by Mark Dever and Paul Alexander (Wheaton, IL: Crossway, 2005). I encourage ministers to put into practice the first chapter's "Four P's": *preach, pray,* build *personal* discipling relationships, and be *patient.* Unless something about a church absolutely must be changed, do not implement any changes your first year. Give yourself time to learn about the congregation and community, and lay a solid foundation by preaching God's Word and seeking the Spirit's leading through prayer.

You may be from a small town and called to serve in an urban church, a church of a different ethnic background from your own, or be at a different life stage from many in the congregation. The major differences you may have with those whom you serve fall under one of three categories: cultural differences, demographic differences, and theological differences.

Cultural Differences

During my first year in North Dakota I returned from a conference with another young pastor who had also lived in an urban part of the country. During the whole drive, we went back and forth, sharing differences we had observed, including the saying, "I suppose a guy could." This phrase is used by some in our neck of the woods as a preface to offering advice without being too direct. My friend's animated response was, "Who's 'the guy'? Am I 'the guy'? Are you 'the guy'? Who's 'the guy'!"

This is an example of a *cultural difference*. Cultural differences can be anything from words that hold unique meanings in one part of the country, to local delicacies, to how you spend your free time, to what you value. For example, in my current context, it is important to know who you are talking to when you use terms like "dinner" or "supper"; else you might miss a meal—or worse, insult your neighbor.

To faithfully pastor those who are culturally different from you, the first thing you should do is learn as much as you can about your context. Start by getting to know the people in your church. If possible, visit them in their homes and places of work. But also learn who your neighbors are. Talk to local business owners. See if the local library has any information on your community. Ask lots of questions. In general, people take pride in their heritage and are more than willing to talk about it. Ask a longtime community member in the church to show you around and introduce you to others.

Learn as much as you can about your context by getting involved. During my first couple years in North Dakota, I rode a combine with a farmer, fixed a fence with one rancher, inoculated and weighed cattle with another, and went fishing with many. This enabled me to build discipling relationships with them, show my love for them, and gain hands-on experience about the values of the community where God called me to serve. Spending time with people on their turf and serving their families in times of need (such as the death of a loved one) earned me capital in their eyes, and then they were willing to trust me in leading the church.

Once you have an idea of the cultural makeup of your community, research those cultural distinctives. Such differences often relate to ethnic backgrounds. For example, our area of North Dakota is made up largely of Germans and Scandinavians who tend to be hard-working and unwilling to ask for help. While hard work is a good thing, self-sufficiency and an unwillingness to open up your life to others hinders personal maturity and being able to serve one other in the Lord. One way this had taken root in the church I serve was in prayer requests. Members tended to seek prayer for physical needs, like health issues—theirs or others'—but not for their own spiritual needs. My wife and I set out to model being open about our spiritual needs and struggles. Over time, longtime church members began seeking prayer for their spiritual needs too.

Paul wrote in 1 Corinthians 9:22, "I have become all things to all men so that by all possible means I might save some."[1] He modeled understanding the cultural differences of his context by, for example, having Timothy circumcised for the sake of ministry among the Jews (Acts 16:3) and appealing to the Athenians' own religion as a bridge to sharing the gospel (Acts 17:22–23). Likewise, it is important for us to pursue pastoral ministry as missionaries. We should desire to learn all we can about our context so God can use us most effectively in it.

Demographic Differences

How do you lead those who are older than you and in many cases have been Christians longer than you've been alive? How do you build consistent disciple-making relationships with guys who work on a twelve-hour rotating shift? These are the kinds of questions I've wrestled with in learning how to pastor those with *demographic differences.* Such factors include age, life stage, family size, income, blue-collar-versus-white-collar or rural-versus-urban mind-set, and the like.

In God's good providence, I had a close friend who had grown up in rural South Dakota and a seminary professor who had pastored in North Dakota. Both provided valuable insights into how to think through these demographic differences before I even moved to the Northern Plains. The two of them helped me understand more clearly the difference between a rural and urban mind-set. For example, in general those in a rural setting have more time

---

1. Scripture quotations in this chapter are from The Holy Bible, New International Version®, NIV®. Copyright © 1973, 1978, 1984 by Biblica, Inc.™ Used by permission. All rights reserved worldwide.

than money, while those in an urban setting often have more money than time.

Ministry strategies are by no means uniform from context to context. What works in an urban context may not work in a small town, and vice versa. The church I was part of in the Chicago area was in a university town and was composed mainly of people with at least a bachelor's degree, if not a master's or doctorate. Many were working toward advanced degrees. You could offer a Sunday school class or men's group using a systematic theology as curriculum and have no problem getting enough participation.

But that was not the case when I arrived in Underwood. The congregation was by no means illiterate or uneducated; reading works of theology just had never been part of their discipleship. I started out slowly. When I found helpful articles from Christian magazines, I would make them available to the congregation. When I found a good deal on a solid book, I would buy it as a Christmas present for church families. Over time, this practice increased their interest in reading. More importantly, it increased their growth as disciples.

The great thing about disciple making is this: it isn't based on a particular demographic but can be tailored to your specific situation. In a suburban church you may have a fruitful men's prayer breakfast at 6:00 a.m., but if I tried that in Underwood, no one would show up. That's not because the guys aren't interested; it's because they are tending to chores around the farm or they're on rotating shift work at that time. I've had to learn the rhythms of life in a rural community to organize ministry for maximum effectiveness. (We don't schedule an event for "deer season opener" at the beginning of November!) But it has also enabled me to do more one-on-one discipling and marriage counseling during times when people are not tied up with their nine-to-five jobs. You need to learn the rhythms of life of your community and adjust to them.

Theological Differences

Much could be said about *theological differences*, but I want to focus more on how to navigate nonessentials and preferences. I do not think anyone in our congregation, with the possible exception of my wife, agrees with me completely on every theological point. For example, we have Calvinists and Arminians, dispensationalists and at least one (me!) who holds to historic premillennialism. And I am thankful not everyone holds the same view on secondary issues, because it has provoked great discussions. I want members' convictions to come from Scripture, not from me.

What I mean by *theological preferences* includes everything from worship style to service length and pastoral expectations. Since I came from a younger, suburban church, a "pastoral visit" sounded to me like getting called into the principal's office. You were either in trouble or going to be asked to do something. But I found that instead of being scary, pastoral visits were how I could learn about my congregation. They were a means by which I could disciple and counsel. In particular, they were a great way to disciple some of our older members who couldn't always make it on Sunday.

My philosophy of ministry is largely based on Ephesians 4:11–12: "[God] gave some to be . . . pastors and teachers, *to prepare God's people for works of service*, so that the body of Christ may be built up." But I also learned that in past generations, especially in small-town churches, the pastor usually did most of the actual ministry. Until I had laid the foundation of the priesthood of all believers, when someone from the church would suggest a new ministry, I would respond by inviting him to go along. This gave me an additional opportunity to disciple that person and show him that he is able to minister too.

Second Timothy 2:24–25 says: "And the Lord's servant must not quarrel; instead, he must be kind to everyone, able to teach, not resentful. Those who oppose him he must gently instruct, in the hope that God will grant them repentance leading them to a knowledge of the truth." If Paul commanded this patient attitude toward the false teachers in Ephesus, I think we can also apply it to those with whom we differ in theological preferences. It's easy to see areas where people need to grow, but I've sought to model and encourage others to look for the areas where God's grace is active and where they're further along and can teach us.

Called and Equipped

So whether God calls you to serve a church that's culturally, demographically, or theologically different from you, or a mix of all three, you should keep a few things in mind.

First, every pastor is interim. You will move, retire, or die, but those who are part of the church and live in that community will remain. So be humble and discerning in the areas you expect the church to adjust to you and where you should adjust to the church.

Second, remember that whatever God calls you to, he will equip you for. If you've only lived in a small town and he calls you to an urban church, he will supply you with everything needful to thrive there.

Finally, if you have a family, don't forget that you are not the only one who will be encountering differences. Be intentional in helping them also to understand and think through what it means to pastor those who are different from you.

5

How to Follow My Lead Pastor When We Disagree

Matt Capps

What do you do when you disagree significantly with the lead pastor of the church you serve? Situations like this often strike unexpectedly, and seminary usually does not teach you how to handle them. We live in a fallen world and understand that relational conflict is often inevitable, even among pastors.

I was eight years into my local church ministry when this situation arose. During a time of transition, I came to see that my ministry philosophy and a few other convictions, such as the end times and preferred Bible translations, were going to greatly affect my ability to serve in that church with a clear conscience. Thankfully, I was able to discuss my concerns and disagreements with the senior leadership, and after much prayer and counsel from other wise brothers, I decided it was best for the church and me to part ways graciously.

In making this decision, I did not always handle things perfectly. Thankfully, my relationship with that church's leadership remains healthy, and we have maintained a mutual respect despite our differences. However, learning to navigate such disagreements was stressful. I pray this chapter will give you a framework to help work through similar differences.

Biblical Appeals for Conflict

An overarching biblical principle is that disagreements should be handled with wisdom and discernment so as not to cause division within the church family. Biblically governed unity is a precious reality for the health of a congregation, so crucial that Jesus devoted much of his High Priestly Prayer in John 17 to the "oneness" of the church. Moreover, Paul is clear in 1 Corinthians 1:10 that there should be no division within the church, but all should be united in one mind. Therefore, we must approach disagreements with humility (Phil. 2:3) and also be "eager to maintain the unity of the Spirit in the bond of peace" (Eph. 4:3).

There is a sense of urgency in the command to live at peace with one another (Rom. 12:18; Heb. 12:14). If conflict is not dealt with or handled appropriately, it will surface later with greater fury and may result in bitterness and division. In this sense, conflict can be an opportunity for us to turn to God, but also for God to work in our hearts and through one another for our good and his glory.

If disagreements are reconcilable, you should aim for relational restoration and peaceful unity (2 Cor. 13:11). In my own experience, many disagreements with other pastors have been solved by honest, grace-filled discussions that seek understanding. Such disagreements stemmed from misunderstandings, and I was passing judgment in ignorance or with partial understanding. In some cases the disagreement remained, but conversation and further reflection allowed me to understand the other person's perspective and lessened the weight of my initial concern. However, some disagreements are not only real but also irreconcilable. How, then, do we decide whether a disagreement is irreconcilable, and what is a wise course of action?

Pastoral Advice for Conflict

If you are a church leader, you understand that everyone sees through the glass darkly (1 Cor. 13:12). Moreover, you understand that the heart is deceitful above all things (Jer. 17:9). You also understand the implications of our sinfulness (Rom. 7:18–25). One of those implications is that conflicts often arise from the passions that war within us (James 4:1–3). Therefore, it is helpful to ask some initial questions concerning the nature and level of importance of your disagreements. This, more than any other consideration, should be your starting point. Consider your disagreement: is this really a hill on which to die?

Looking back, I realize that I did not always take that question into consideration when I should have. Depravity not only affects our ability to think clearly but also can lead us to respond inappropriately with our emotions and actions. In light of this, here are some things I've learned about how best to handle such situations. Ask yourself these questions:

1. *Is the disagreement over a personal offense?* If so, how serious is it? Jesus warned of the connection between our forgiving those who have sinned against us and his forgiveness of us (Matt. 6:14–15; Mark 11:25). It's not that you earn God's forgiveness by forgiving; no, God expects forgiven people to forgive (Matt. 18:21–35). In the same way, the offender should seek resolution and restoration (Rom. 12:18).

In some cases, the offender may be in simple or willful ignorance. The reason for the ignorance may be mitigating circumstances or a hardened heart. While differing reasons may require different approaches in dealing with the offender and our disagreement, the central truth of Matthew 18:15 stands: "If your brother sins against you, go and tell him his fault, between you and him alone. If he listens to you, you have gained your brother."

You owe it to one another to follow the biblical pattern; this is what Christian love requires. Whether or not the disagreement involves a personal offense, talking face-to-face to clarify the situation should always be our starting point.

When leaders are unwilling to follow the biblical pattern of resolution and restoration, disagreements do not go well. This happens when either the offending or the offended party is unwilling to identify the source of conflict or is unwilling to pursue restoration. It's important to understand the context in which Jesus gives us the process for conflict resolution in Matthew 18:15–20. In the paragraph before, he paints a picture of a shepherd who searches for a lost sheep and rejoices when he finds it (Matt. 18:12–14). In verses 21–35, Jesus tells the story of the unmerciful servant, which instructs us to be merciful as God has shown us mercy. The steps to conflict resolution are sandwiched between images of a good shepherd bringing home a lost sheep and a call to show others mercy.

If there is unwillingness to seek resolution or restoration on either side, it may be necessary to approach the other party with one or two witnesses (Matt. 18:16). At each stage of Matthew 18:15–17, clarifying questions are important for better understanding the disagreement.

2. *Is the disagreement related to ministry philosophy, and if so, at* *what level?* Admittedly, this is often one is the most complex areas of disagreement, since it involves both doctrine and wisdom. It is unwise to work with a lead pastor when you seriously disagree over ministry philosophy. Because of the lead pastor's role in a ministry structure, it is unlikely you will effect change in a healthy way unless the two of you compromise or enact change together.

There must be a reasonable chance you can successfully bring about change for you to justify continuing to serve under his leadership. A disagreement at the level of ministry philosophy might well compel you to leave your current position and minister in a more appropriate context. Such a change might be for the long-term good of both the church and your own conscience. Unfortunately, if you feel the integrity of the gospel is at stake, your disagreement is likely irreconcilable, and it's best to seek a wise course to part ways.

3. *Is the disagreement over a failure to carry out biblically pre-* *scribed ministry patterns?* You might reach a place where you be-

lieve the lead pastor is not fulfilling his pastoral role as established in Scripture. In the New Testament, the title *pastor* often carries the connotations of "shepherd" (Eph. 4:11; Heb. 13:20; 1 Pet. 2:25). The pastor feeds, nurtures, and protects the flock. *Elder* speaks to the spiritual maturity needed for the office as leaders function as representatives of the church (Acts 14:21–23). *Overseer* indicates a function of providing leadership and direction for the church (1 Tim. 3:1–7; 1 Pet. 5:1–3). The pastor's primary focus should be leading (1 Thess. 5:12; Heb. 13:17), caring for (James 5:14; 1 Pet. 5:2), teaching/preaching (Eph. 4:11; 1 Tim. 3:2; 5:17; Titus 1:9), and equipping the saints for the work of the ministry (Eph. 4:12–16; 2 Tim. 2:2).

If the lead pastor is unwilling to function within the biblical pattern, it may be time for him to leave. Sadly, too many lead pastors operate as if they are the only ones who hear from God ("I am God's man"), which excuses them from accountability to their own church or pastoral staff.

4. *Is the disagreement a doctrinal matter?* If so, at what level? There are different levels at which you must organize the importance of doctrine. Albert Mohler's three levels of "theological triage" are helpful to visualize and assess these differences.[1]

First-order doctrines are the absolutes that define core beliefs of the Christian faith—the authority of Scripture, the Trinity, man, and salvation (justification by faith) are first-order doctrines. These are most central to the Christian faith. If the difference revolves around one of these doctrines, it is best to part ways.

Second-order doctrines focus on convictions that do not represent core Christian beliefs. These issues may have significant influence on the church's health and effectiveness. Second-level doctrines include denominational distinctives or core values peculiar to specific churches—baptism, church government, women in ministry, and so on. A local church needs agreement in theory and practice on these matters. In significant ways, second-order issues

---

1. See Albert Mohler, "A Call for Theological Triage and Christian Maturity," *Church History*, July 12, 2005, http://www.albertmohler.com/2005/07/12/a-call-for-theological-triage-and-christian-maturity/.

shape church direction and fellowship. When differences arise on these matters, it would likely be best to part ways for one's own integrity and also for the health of that church.

Third-order doctrines include issues over which good Christians may disagree without division. These are less-clear biblical issues that generally are not worth dividing over, including issues such as eschatology. Christians may disagree over any number of particulars related to the interpretation of difficult end-times texts, but these differences should not cause separation. If the lead pastor, however, takes a third-level doctrine or matter of conscience and imposes it on the church as a matter of first importance, it may be best to part ways.

The failure to rightly measure disagreement in terms of importance is one of the main reasons conflicts among elders erupt. If *every* disagreement ranks at the level of gospel importance, then there's no margin for fallibility among brothers. If *no* issue is regarded as of first importance, then there's no accountability. Therefore, thinking through these issues with clarity, wisdom, and humility is important as one seeks a wise course of action.

Ecclesiological Structures for Peacemaking

Thankfully, regardless of your denomination or ecclesiology, there are usually policies, processes, and structures in place to frame your response when conflict arises. Episcopalians can seek the guidance of a bishop during conflict; Presbyterians have the session, the presbytery, and church courts; and congregational churches usually put in place structures for dealing with conflict such as elders/deacons or personnel teams to provide a nonpartisan perspective. When there is no such structure, tragedy is certain to follow.

Sometimes even ecclesiological structures fail to solve staff conflicts. One elder friend recently faced a situation in which the lead pastor was stealing sermons word-for-word from a prominent preacher's published manuscripts. The pastor was using illustrations from the book and changing the names of people involved to personalize the stories as if they had happened to him. My friend approached the chairman of the deacons and the personnel committee once the evidence was undeniable. Sadly, the pastor denied the claims, stating he had never seen the works he was plagiarizing. Neither the deacons nor the personnel committee held him accountable, and my friend quickly transitioned to another place of ministry.

Even with ecclesiological structures in place to deal with disagreements, it's possible any avenue will be considered divisive or disloyal. The lead pastor may be tempted to use his position to sideline the disagreement by leveling charges of destroying unity or insubordination. But if the church has been vigilant to put appropriate procedures in place to deal with conflict pertaining to the lead pastor, there is hope for reconciliation.

A Way Forward

The first step in dealing with conflict with a lead pastor or another leader is to pray for humility and repentance. In most cases, it is wise to seek the input of other trusted counselors before you plan to resolve the disagreement. You must always be open to the possibility that you have misunderstood, that the other elder is in the right, and that your thinking needs to adjust.

In Matthew 7:3, Jesus challenges us by asking, "Why do you see the speck that is in your brother's eye, but do not notice the log that is in your own eye?" At times our desires and expectations so control us, we fail to see the log in our own eye, and we blow up over the speck in someone else's.

Then, having prayerfully examined yourself, go privately to the lead pastor and, remembering you may not see the whole situation, give him the benefit of the doubt. After patiently hearing your pastor's explanation or understanding of the disagreement, you may find that you still disagree. If this happens and the disagreement is not central to the faith, humbly accept that you see things differently and resolve to keep your disagreement to yourself.

Always be aware of the lurking danger of divisive and harmful gossip that could arise in conversations with other staff and church members. Be willing to quickly and humbly confess and repent of all your sin in the disagreement. Seek ways to honor your pastor any way you can, both publicly and privately. The ninth commandment requires you to do all you can to uphold his reputation with others.

The process in Matthew 18 seems to indicate that the goal is to keep the circle as small as possible, for as long as possible, to help resolve the conflict. If the conflict can be resolved early in this process, there is usually no need to go public with the matter.

There are cases, however, when disagreements and sinful practices should be made public. For example, if a church leader is doing something against the law, disclosure and involvement of civil authorities is needed. Pastors should seek to minister in adherence to proper legal and ethical requirements in all situations.

Conclusion

The best rule of thumb is to ask yourself how to love your pastor as you would want to be loved in each situation. At each step of dealing with a disagreement, ask how you would want to be handled by a staff member if you needed correction. It is also helpful to consider your experience, tenure, and position in the church. While seminary can equip you to understand and apply biblical truth concerning conflict resolution, it cannot ready you personally to respond in a way that honors God, especially when your emotions are stirred. In many cases, patiently reflecting on relational conflict is the furnace that forges wisdom. Typically, there is a notable difference in the way an experienced associate pastor would handle a disagreement with a lead pastor and the way a twenty-year-old first-time youth pastor would.

In rare cases, you may disagree so strongly with the lead pastor, or your disagreement may concern such a grave matter, that it will hinder you from wholeheartedly submitting to his leadership and serving with him. Where this is the case, it is best to leave after discussing your intent with him.

In my own case, this worked out for the good of my ministry and my maturity as a young pastor. Not long ago, I was able to sit down and thank the pastor who helped me see it was time to move on from the ministry role I held at the church he led. Leaving was painful at the time, and I didn't fully understand it. However, looking back, I see that it was for my good and the good of that church. Our vulnerability in that process forged a relationship that wouldn't have otherwise existed.

In the context of love and trust, being vulnerable in resolving conflict gets to the heart of the issue quickly. It also clarifies motivations that may have led to such conflict, leaving nothing to the imagination. When two people are vulnerable with each another in conflict, they can move toward one another with grace, thereby demonstrating the power of the gospel.

In one sense, Scripture's redemption story is a history of conflict and resolution. The greatest conflict the world has ever known was settled on the cross. At Calvary, God moved toward us with mercy and grace to resolve the conflict between our sin and his holiness. As Matthew demonstrates, the goal of all conflict resolution is restoration. Those who have been redeemed by God and restored to God, must demonstrate the power of the gospel by resolving conflict and seeking restoration with one another.

The hope of the gospel is that God can redeem every hardship we face, including interpersonal conflict, for good purposes. Whatever lies ahead, know that nothing in all creation can separate you from God's love for you in Christ (Rom. 8:31–39); allow that truth to anchor your soul as you move forward with wisdom and grace.

6

How to Lead My Leaders

Juan Sanchez

"What concerns you most about becoming our pastor?" That was one of the questions posed to me the first time I met with elders of a church that was seeking a pastor. It was a valid question. The former pastor was under church discipline; the elders were learning what it meant to be elders; and while they had about fifteen hundred members on the roll, their Sunday morning attendance had dwindled to about 350 people. Add to all that the fact that they were carrying an overwhelming debt load they could not service. There were many concerns, but which one would rise above the rest? Without hesitation I replied, "The leadership."

Our Lord Jesus has structured his church for his mission (Eph. 4:11–16) and charged male leaders, called elders, to care for his flock until his return (1 Pet. 5:1–5). Such leadership is vital to the church's mission. If the elders of a church are of one mind, one heart, and one voice, then, by God's grace, they will be able to withstand whatever conflicts and crises may arise. However, if the elders are divided, then it wouldn't matter how well things may appear to be going for the church; its leaders will eventually wreak conflict and possibly destroy an already weakened church.

Sadly, I didn't learn this lesson in seminary. It took a difficult situation when the leadership was not united to help me understand the importance of leadership in the church, and the importance of leading other leaders. Consequently, leadership had become my main concern when the elders asked me that question; and leadership remains my main concern today. Since my seminary days, I have learned that if I am to lead the church and its leaders well, I must first have a biblical understanding of leadership. Then I must not only model that biblical leadership for those around me but also expect the same from others in the church.

Defining Biblical Leadership

Without a biblical understanding of leadership, we may be tempted either to surrender our authority through passivity and fear of man, thus harming those under our care, or to abuse our authority through manipulative or oppressive means, thus serving ourselves. This distortion of leadership was evident in the garden when Adam embraced passivity and failed to lead Eve away from temptation (Gen. 3:6). And it became a settled reality when Eve was cursed with the certainty that as a result of the fall, Adam would oppress her in response to her desire for his leadership (Gen. 3:16).

Scripture in its entirety depicts this ongoing struggle between godly leadership and distorted leadership. It's true in the male-female marriage relationship, and it's also true in the church, where we are called to reflect biblical patterns of leadership (1 Tim. 2:11–15). So what does biblical leadership look like? How may we define it?

I suspect most evangelical leaders are accustomed to John Maxwell's definition of leadership as "influence." In "The Maxwell Fallacy: There's More to Leadership Than Influence," leadership guru David Burkus takes issue with this overly simplistic definition, because it leaves the door open to influence through coercion, manipulation, or threat. That's not biblical leadership. Instead, Burkus proposes that "leadership is the process of influencing others to work toward a mutually desired vision."[1]

This clarification is helpful. Thankfully, for church leaders, our mutually desired vision is spelled out in Scripture. The church is to display the manifold wisdom of God to the cosmic powers as we proclaim "the unsearchable riches of Christ" and "bring to light for everyone" God's eternal plan to exalt Christ as Lord over all things (Eph. 3:8–10). The question remains: How do we influence the church and its leaders to display the manifold wisdom of God as we proclaim the gospel and call people to repentance and faith and a life of obedience to King Jesus?

Credibility

I have come to realize that an oft-neglected component of biblical leadership is credibility. We rightly emphasize *character* (1 Tim. 3; Titus 1); we rightly emphasize *competency* (ability to teach); and we rightly expect *care* for the congregation (1 Peter 5). Yet we often fail to consider that it takes time for character, competency, and care to be observed to the point that *credibility* is established. Mike Ayers, writing at *For the Church*, defines credibility as the "moral permission for the [leader] in question to exercise influence."[2] Credibility is required of all leaders, including the leader of other leaders. So how do you build credibility among those you lead?

When Jesus structured his church for mission (Eph. 4:11–16), he emphasized the priority of the ministry of the Word. When Paul addressed leadership issues in the churches, he prioritized character over gifting (1 Tim. 3:1–8; Titus 1:5–8). When Peter described the role of the church's leaders, he stressed the importance of care for the congregation motivated by love rather than compulsion.

As we consider this panorama of biblical descriptions and qualifications of leadership, a biblical understanding of leadership emerges. Biblical leaders are men of godly *character* who display a

---

1. David Barkus, "The Maxwell Fallacy: There's More to Leadership Than Influence," *Change This*, March 9, 2011, http://changethis.com/manifesto/show/80.05.MaxwellFallacy.

2. Mike Ayers, "The Stewardship of Power," *For the Church*, May 23, 2016, http://ftc.co/resource-library/blog-entries/the-stewardship-of-power.

sufficient *competency* in handling the Word of God and who express a loving *care* for the flock of God among them. As leadership candidates display biblical *character*, faithful *competency*, and loving *care* over time, they will establish *credibility* with the congregation that makes them worthy of following.

Think of biblical leadership as follows:

$$\frac{\text{Character} + \text{Competency} + \text{Care}}{\text{Time}} = \text{Credibility}$$

Laying the Foundation

When I came to High Pointe Baptist Church in Austin, Texas, the church and its leaders gave me the benefit of the doubt. Sure, they performed criminal and financial background checks, requested personal references, and checked my credentials, but they trusted all those sources. Over time, I had to show I was the person they believed me to be. They needed to see for themselves I was a man of godly character; they needed to see I was sufficiently competent to teach; they needed to see I was caring enough to shepherd the church faithfully. This observation takes time.

But there is something a pastor can do immediately to begin laying a proper leadership foundation at the church: consecutive expositional preaching. Biblical authority is a derived authority; it is not intrinsic to our personality, our gifting, our credentials, or anything else of human origins. When we model faithful handling of God's Word, this increases listeners' confidence in the Bible, and their confidence in our competency to handle Scripture will grow. Faithful exposition week in and week out models character, competency, and care for the congregation. This is an important foundation for leadership in the church and the leadership of other leaders.

Expecting Biblical Leadership

It should come as no surprise that if we are going to lead others well, we have to be credible leaders ourselves. Not only is the church watching; other leaders are watching us too. But soon, rather than later, we need to expect others to display and practice biblical leadership. Since seminary, I've learned three important lessons that help me to lead other leaders.

1. Identify and Invite Biblical Leaders

I remember asking a well-respected church planter in our area to reflect on his early mistakes and share with me what he would do differently. Without hesitation he said, "I would be slower in bringing new elders on board." It's good and healthy to want to share the leadership burden, but too often we are tempted to bring on men who are not qualified or ready.

It's okay to go slow in identifying leaders (1 Tim. 5:22). It's better to bring on new leaders slowly than to have to remove leaders who are not qualified, competent, or caring. In fact, unqualified men are most difficult to lead, and they're the most likely to create trouble.

I remember once, during a difficult congregational meeting at a previous church, I had just finished explaining the church-discipline process from Matthew 18 and 1 Corinthians 5. We had already gone through this teaching with the church's recognized leaders, but as soon as I had explained the importance and necessity of church discipline, a deacon rose and said, "I don't know about what you just said, but here's how I feel..."

Feel? Yes, he actually said "feel"! This brother, who had heard this teaching before, became overwhelmed by the fear of man at the public meeting, and so he caved. He showed that he did not care for the congregation; he cared only for himself.

This is the kind of thing you want to find out before someone is recognized as a church leader. Be sure to work through healthy biblical processes that help identify godly, biblically qualified leaders. Then invite them to serve alongside you.

At High Pointe, we are constantly on the lookout for men who have godly character and faithfully love the congregation. We expect that they are regularly sharing the gospel with unbelievers and diligently discipling other men. We expect them to be faithfully engaged in congregational life. And we expect they would do all these things whether or not they were officially recognized by the church as leaders. When men like this show up on our radar, we give them opportunities to teach publicly, and we observe and evaluate their teaching competency. During our elders' meetings, we review a list of such potential men who seem to be on a trajectory to becoming elders, and we pray that God will grant us wisdom in nominating future elders.

Once a brother's name is on most or all of our lists, we ask him about his interest in serving as an elder. If he shows interest, he fills out a questionnaire that focuses mainly on the biblical qualifications of eldership. The elders review the questionnaires, and if we're in agreement, we invite him for a thorough interview. If all parties agree to continue, we invite the prospect to sit in our meeting up until the "elders only" time. Then we ask him to choose an elder to mentor him. During our time together, the candidate not only observes how we care for the congregation; he also observes the character, competency, and care of the elders.

You may wonder what all this has to do with leading leaders. Think about it: it is easier to lead brothers who are biblically qualified and united in mind, heart, and voice, than those who aren't. At High Pointe, the elder nomination process is a means by which we protect the congregation in advance from unbiblical leadership. When we work hard to find faithful men who love Christ, love the gospel, and love the church, we have a better likelihood of having a team of leaders who know when to lead and when to follow for the good of the church. Never assume without evidence that someone is qualified for biblical leadership—you will live to regret it. And don't imagine biblical leadership will spring up down the road simply because you put someone in a position. Instead, expect biblical leadership to manifest itself from the beginning as you identify and invite brothers to join church leadership.

2. Equip and Empower Biblical Leaders

If you want to frustrate other leaders and create leadership conflicts in the church, invite them to lead but don't equip them or empower them to lead. Sometimes authoritarian leaders recognize other leaders' readiness to serve alongside them, but merely as rubber stamps for what the pastor wants to do. These recruits are elders in name only. Real leaders will not last long under such circumstances. But we have to realize that well-meaning pastors sometimes frustrate other leaders this way. It starts with the prideful assumption that the pastor can do things better and faster than those assigned to certain tasks. Rather than taking the time to equip other leaders and empower them for their ministries, we merely do them ourselves. But if we cannot trust other leaders to fulfill their assignments, why do we invite them to lead in the first place?

We need to view leadership with a long-term perspective. We are raising up and equipping leaders for the future, when we're gone, so let's equip them and empower them to lead now, while we have the ability to encourage and shape their leadership.

Equipping should happen all the time. At High Pointe, we are constantly reading books together, talking together, praying together, and training together. But you must do more than equip and train leaders; at some point, you have to let them lead and give them the room to fail.

Empowering leaders begins with encouraging their full participation in decision-making conversations and processes. During our conversations, each elder is free and encouraged to contribute, ask questions, and provide suggestions. If consensus is clear, we move forward; if not, we vote. The majority rules, even when I'm in the minority.

We should also encourage our leaders to lead in their areas of strength and gifting. Because of my public preaching ministry, it's clear to the congregation that I'm the primary leader of the church. So it's up to me to continually remind the congregation about the plural leadership of our church. It's up to me to give credit, recognize, and honor other leaders for leading well. It's up to me to allow other elders to lead privately and publicly. Our elders' meetings are led by our chairman, not me; our members' meetings are moderated by our chairman or vice chairman, not me; our pastoral prayer is given by one of our staff pastors, not me; our Sunday evening preaching is done by one of our elders or pastoral staff, not normally me. Good leaders give credit away and take responsibility upon themselves. I've learned to equip and empower other leaders to lead according to their gifting and strengths.

3. Evaluate Biblical Leadership

Perhaps the most crucial way I've learned to lead others is through evaluation. Proper evaluation requires a culture where constructive criticism and healthy encouragement are given in honest humility and received with honest gratitude. As the primary leader, I am responsible for establishing and cultivating this atmosphere by modeling constructive criticism and healthy encouragement and also allowing myself to be evaluated by other leaders. For our pastoral staff, this evaluation happens at our weekly service review. We normally meet at a local coffee shop on Monday afternoons, and we review the entire Sunday, including my sermon. This process not only helps me to grow as a preacher; it also communicates to the other leaders that it is safe to ask questions of me and criticize me. I cannot overemphasize how valuable this time is for me personally as a leader, and for our leadership team as a whole.

But we also perform evaluations of everything we do as a church. Nothing is off the table, even when it comes to my leadership. Our meeting agenda includes opportunities for the other elders to share things they see at High Pointe that are encouraging and things that are concerning. These conversations allow us to evaluate our ministry together and ask questions of each other, depending on who is leading a particular ministry being evaluated.

There are also times when another elder and I will sit down with members of our pastoral staff for formal evaluations. We evaluate character, competency, and care for the congregation. Having these evaluations is particularly important for our young men pursuing pastoral ministry. It allows them to learn to receive honest criticism and healthy encouragement with humility. If they are unable to receive such criticism and encouragement with humility, it becomes clear to us that they are either not ready for pastoral ministry or perhaps not qualified for the pastorate.

Seminary of the Local Church

I thank God for my time in seminary. Seminary is not designed to teach you everything, and seminary cannot teach you what only the local church must teach you. After thirty years of pastoral ministry, I've learned many things in the "seminary" of the local church. Many of those lessons have come as a result of my youth, impatience, and hardheadedness.

But I am thankful for loving congregations who have cared well for me and my family and who forgave me early on for my youthful missteps. One of the most important lessons I've learned in the church is that leadership matters. If I am to lead others well, then I need to have a biblical understanding of leadership myself, and then I need to work diligently to lay a proper foundation for biblical leadership. But that's not enough. As some point, I need to expect biblical leadership of those around me.

7

How to Raise My Kids to Love the Church

Matt McCullough

Most Friday mornings my small boys and I go for a hike in one of the state parks within easy driving distance of our city. One of our favorites is a spot called the Narrows of the Harpeth. As you might gather from the name, the heart of this park is a narrow strip of land carved out by two stretches of the Harpeth River as it curves back toward itself after a tight bend, nearly closing a circle. For millennia after millennia, two parallel lengths of the river have eroded what was once a hill between them into a steep bluff overlooking, on each side, a separate portion of the Harpeth River below.

I've never actually measured the distance from one side of this bluff to the other, but in some places it's not much wider than the path that runs along the top—I'd guess no more than fifteen or twenty feet across. On either side is a sheer rock-wall drop of several hundred feet. It's a treacherous path. You have to be careful and stay right in the middle. A step away from the danger on one side is a step toward danger on the other.

This path is how I imagine the line I'm trying to walk as the pastor of a church I love and the parent of kids I love, whom I desperately want to see love the church themselves. I want to do everything I can do to help my children love the church, but to my eyes the path forward runs between dangerous cliffs on two sides.

Two Cliffs, Two Dangers

I want to describe these two metaphorical cliffs as I see them and offer some practical suggestions about how to avoid them. But first let me explain where I'm coming from.

In 2010 my wife and I welcomed our first child the same year we helped plant our church. I've been a parent for roughly the same length of time I've been a pastor, and that isn't very long. But it didn't take long to recognize that the strain on a pastor's family life isn't just an old cliché—or to see why the burned-over, hell-raising pastor's kid is more than an empty stereotype. In what follows I'll be drawing more from what I'm hoping to do with my kids than what I have done already.

That said, I'm also writing from another sort of experience—not from my experience as a pastor, with lessons learned the hard way, but from my experience as a pastor's kid. I grew up in a pastor's family. I'm giving my life to the local church now because I came to love it under the ministry of my father. The advice I offer below comes from what I saw him model and what I've seen bear fruit in my life.

Now back to the metaphorical cliffs. On one side, we have to avoid treating the local church like a job that is bracketed off from our private lives. Pastoring a church is far more to us than a source of income. Put positively, if we want our kids to love the church, we have to show them that we love the church ourselves—that we believe it is worth the investment of our whole lives.

And yet, on the other side, we have to avoid letting the burdens of ministry infiltrate the time and attention our families deserve. Put positively, we can help our kids by protecting our relationship with them from the church—removing unnecessary obstacles that could make the church more difficult to love than it should be.

1. We Must Show Our Kids That We Love the Church

The Bible describes the local church as the engine of God's work in the world. It is a kingdom of people who want to honor and serve God as King in all of life (Matthew 16, 18, 28). It is a family of those adopted by God and bound to one another by his love (Ephesians 2). It is a body in which everyone encounters everything together (1 Corinthians 12). It is not some sort of subscription service where you affiliate so it's always there in case you need it. Our connection to the local church isn't voluntary. It isn't selective. It's fundamental, life-shaping, and all-encompassing.

We must teach our kids these truths from the Bible. But just as important is what we show them. No one will have a better view of how closely our words about the church match our posture toward the church. We can't teach our kids to love the church unless they can see that we actually love the church.

Perhaps the most important thing we can do to demonstrate our love for the church is to crucify any trace of careerism. The local church doesn't exist to provide us with jobs. It is nobody's employer. It is so much bigger than any one of us and what we may accomplish. The local church must be the people you share life with and belong to before it is the place you go to work.

If we treat our churches like commodities that bring value to our lives, meet our needs, or fill our ambitions—like a plasma TV or a five-bedroom house or a best-in-class SUV—we will always be evaluating them against the options of elsewhere. We will hold them at arm's length for detached observation. Or we'll keep them under our microscope where every flaw is obvious, prompting us to wonder what might be different in some other church.

Our kids will take their cues from us. If we emit even a whiff of careerism, they'll smell it. If they sense from us that the church we serve is a rung on a ladder we're still climbing, they will hold themselves back. The church will remain a "them" to the family's "us." At worst, they may feel trapped by your job in a church they didn't choose. At best they may bide their time until the next move. But they will struggle to fully identify themselves with your church.

This sense of submission and belonging is one of the greatest gifts my father gave me. He modeled love for the church and its people as our people. He continues to pastor in a place where people joke that if you're not born in the county, you can live there twenty years and not be from there. It's a place where the average tenure in churches is no more than a few years, and where it's normal for pastors' families to live on a separate plane from those they serve. It is a credit to him and to the church that we didn't live that way. He never acted like he wasn't from there. He wasn't an external observer of the culture, as if his life were too big to be contained by this place and its people. Our lives were fully integrated with theirs.

Our kids need to see us approach our work with joy and hope. They need to see us cultivate relationships in the church as genuine, mutual friendships—not as clients or as items on our to-do list. They need to see us engage problems in the church with empathy and loving commitment, never speaking as if the church were something other than all of us.

And, sometimes, the most powerful way to demonstrate our love for the church is to bring our kids into our pastoral work. I'm not suggesting you force them along with you. I'm saying invite them along when they're interested. Maybe it's modeling joyful servant leadership while you help set up for an event. But, depending on the situation, you could also let them observe some of your pastoral work.

Growing up, I lived in a rural community with many elderly members unable to leave their homes. Visiting these members was a big part of my father's ministry, and my dad would often take me with him. He also did a lot of hospital visits, usually more than an hour away. If the circumstances were appropriate, I'd ride along with him on those too. What I got from these ride-along opportunities was much more than quality time with my father, as precious as that was. I got a close look at the gravity of his work—to be with people facing their most difficult seasons, sometimes the worst moments of their lives. I saw people believing on Jesus across a wide range of ages and an even wider range of experiences. I saw them moved by awareness that they were not alone and not forgotten, that they faced life's greatest challenges in solidarity with a people to whom they belonged. And I saw firsthand how much my father loved caring for his people.

2. We Must Protect Our Relationship with Our Kids from the Church

The more sensitive we are about one danger for our kids—seeing the church as merely an employer, an accessory to life rather than its framework—the more susceptible we'll be to another danger. As followers of Jesus, much less pastors, we're called to build our lives around the local church. But we cannot allow our shepherding responsibilities to take over our lives.

The invasiveness of pastoral work is inevitable. By nature, the core tasks involved are never finished. At what point have you prepared "enough" for a sermon? Have you ever delivered one you felt was truly ready? At what point is someone finally and fully discipled? You can't decide when a marriage will face a crisis, or how long it will take to shepherd people through it. The burdens from the care you're giving to your people live in your mind.

We can't keep the responsibilities of ministry from affecting the rhythms of our family lives. And precisely because we can't avoid the creeping presence of these responsibilities, we have to do everything we can to protect from the church our relationship with our kids.

If our children feel like the church is their competition for our time and affection, it will always be difficult for them to love the church. So we have to prove to them in the structures of our normal lives that we prioritize them. The goal is to convince our kids that we're never happier than when we're with them. If they expect that we'd always rather be with them, it will be easier for them to accept those times that we can't be.

How can we protect our kids from the demands of church life? How can we build a family culture where our kids don't have to feel like our church is their competition? Here are a few suggestions that have worked well for me:

1. *Pick a day off and stick to it ruthlessly.* For me that day is Friday. I try to build my week to make that day as carefree as possible. I try to avoid intense counseling sessions on Thursday that I know would weigh on my mind the next day. I make sure I have a rough draft of my sermon written by Thursday evening, and I carve out Saturday afternoons for revision.

That way on Friday I don't feel the pressure to write it, and I know I have the next day to fix it. Do what works for you. But the point is to have a day when your kids can count on having you all to themselves. I find this expectation helps soften the blow of long hours apart from them and lost evenings earlier in the week.

2. *Plan fun family activities on your day off.* We have to resist the urge to think of this day as a chance to veg and recover, much as we might need it. It's an opportunity to disengage from work by engaging with our kids. What this looks like will vary based on the ages of your kids, of course. Because ours are still young and my wife stays home with them all week, I try to get them out of the house.

Unless she wants to weigh in, I take responsibility for planning the day. This is partly a good way to serve my wife—to take at least one thing off her plate or give her some much-needed breathing room. But it also makes a point to our kids: our time together is a priority for me. It's a high point in my week, something we're always looking forward to. When something derails that time, it disappoints me too.

3. *When work intrudes on your family time, communicate as much as you can as clearly as you can.* Much of what we face in our work is private information we can't share with our wives, much less our children. But we need to find acceptable ways to let them know *that* we're weighed down, even if we can't tell them *why*. Don't make your kids wonder whether your seeming quiet or distant is

because you're concerned about a member who's in trouble or is because they've done something to offend you.

And some of the tasks that fall to us will be time sensitive and unpredictable. We can't fully avoid this, but we can at least make it clear to our kids when we're working and when we're with them. If you can't avoid firing off an email or a text during family movie night, tell them what you're doing and put the device away ASAP.

4. *Don't use family time for multitasking.* Speaking of devices, because much of our work involves thinking or communication, the ubiquity of information on our phones or tablets makes the temptation to multitask nearly irresistible. If I have to choose moment by moment what I'm going to engage with, I'll loose the battle too many times.

Find a system that works for you, but you might consider only checking email during designated times. Perhaps even get rid of your phone altogether when you're engaging with your children. When I was a kid, we'd take the landline off the hook and stuff it in a drawer. These days, isolation isn't so straightforward, but a drawer still isn't a bad idea.

5. *Keep the church calendar as slim as possible.* You may not have full control over what goes into your church's programming. But where you have influence, work to keep your calendar slim and simple. If you're away from your family, you don't want it to be about making perfunctory appearances, like some sort of dignitary. You want it to be because you're forced away by things that truly matter.

Pray for Wisdom

It isn't easy to walk the path between the detachment that treats the church as mere employer and the immersion that leaves no clear space for our children. Take a step away from one cliff and you've taken a step closer to the other. We need day-by-day wisdom, more wisdom than we have on our own. We need open communication with our wives about what they're perceiving in us.

We need to expose our lives to our fellow elders and to close friends in our churches. We need to seek out advice from more-seasoned pastors who know how to ask the right questions and recognize the warning signs. In short, to shepherd our kids toward love for the church, we must parent and pastor in community with people who know us and love us enough to be honest about what they see.

Ultimately, though, we can't give our kids love for the local church. That takes supernatural power. When you're familiar with the forms of dysfunction Paul was addressing in the first twelve chapters of 1 Corinthians, you understand why he describes love as he does in chapter 13.

The only love that can sustain a local church is a love that's patient and kind, that isn't easily offended and doesn't hold onto a grudge, that bears with all things and believes the best about others. This sort of love isn't learned behavior. It's a gift of God's grace—a miracle performed by his power in the hearts of his children. In this light, the most fundamental thing we must do for our kids if we want to see them love the church is pray for them.

8

How to Shepherd My Congregation through Seasons of Suffering

John Onwuchekwa

Within my first two years as a pastor, I got a call from the wife of one of my best friends. I'll never forget it. She just found out his little brother had been murdered, and she was struggling with how to give the information to her husband. So she called me. Given this intense weight on my shoulders—one I'd never felt before—I didn't feel prepared.

In a few minutes, that initial weight seemed light, compared with the burden of breaking the news to my friend. It was like replacing a barbell with an anvil. As he cried uncontrollably, I remember thinking I never wanted to feel that kind of pain again. And strangely, as time went on, I forgot that feeling—forgot how heavy it was. It vanished from my mind. Deep down, I felt pain like that would hit other people but, I thought, would stay far from me.

Then came April 14, 2015.

Less than two months from the launch of Cornerstone Church in Atlanta, I was out of town and received a phone call from my mom asking me to check on my brother—she couldn't reach him. It took only a few phone calls for me to learn that my brother, a thirty-two-year-old pastor, was dead. In the best physical shape of his life, he died unexpectedly in his car—alone. He was gone in an instant.

After calling my parents and other three siblings, I sat with the reality that suffering had found me. I was blindsided, unprepared to deal with it. I knew death is part of life. But getting that call was different. I felt it far more deeply than before. All those initial feelings rushed back, more intense than before, coupled with every emotion I felt in the past.

Then, on the day we opened our church doors, hoping to breathe new life into a community, my wife learned her grandmother had died. Over the next three months, suffering spread like a virus through our church. A good friend lost his sister to cancer. Another lost a grandmother. A cousin. A best friend. On and on, and it kept coming.

And then it hit home for us when we buried a member we had baptized a few months prior. It seemed clear to me why David used the phrase "the valley of the shadow of death" in Psalm 23:4. Death stings in an instant, but its shadow of depression lingers like an unwelcome houseguest, far too long.

Unprepared for the Darkness

So here I was, having been a pastor for eight years, once an intensely extroverted optimist, now an introverted hermit struggling with depression, trying to make sure our church didn't drown under the tidal wave of suffering and storm clouds of depression. In spite of advanced Bible degrees, I was unprepared.

I was unprepared because as fallen humans, we eagerly see with crystal clarity things about our future that may never happen to or for us (marriage, the birth of our first child, promotions, notoriety, and so on), but we tend to turn a blind eye to the one prospect that will eventually befall all of us: affliction. We imagine the good as if it's inevitable, but the inevitable is often unimaginable. Yet, when the inevitable comes, will we be prepared to deal with it and lead our churches through it? If seminary doesn't teach you that lesson, I hope this brief chapter will serve as something of a primer.

The words that follow aren't meant to be a how-to guide. Far from it, for no such thing exists when it comes to facing suffering. If anything, these are merely the reflections of a pastor who has learned much from his mistakes. Some lessons can be learned in a classroom, but responding to suffering isn't one of them. This lesson is learned and relearned in the crucible. One of the important things I've learned is that suffering doesn't necessarily give you better words; it only makes you more generous with your tears. I hope that even the thought of leading your church through hard times would soften your heart and humble you. That's the best preparation for leading your sheep through the valley of the shadow of death

Pain Is the Soul's Stimulus to Seeking Peace

I did what we all do when I heard the bad news chronicled above: I searched for peace. I didn't do it explicitly, for you don't say to yourself, *I will search for peace now*—you just seek it. You get busy. You look for relief from pain. You don't just sit back and take it. You may try to ignore it and act like it's not there. You may drown yourself in distractions. You may try anything to forget. But you soon realize that while pleasures are easily forgotten, pain comes with a photographic memory. You remember the smells, the unimportant details, the sense of horror of the place where you were standing, just how weak your knees felt. Sleeping it off doesn't work. In the morning you still long for just one more hug from your lost loved one. The pain is still there.

I wish I could say that going through suffering equips you with better answers for people on this quest for peace, but that isn't necessarily true. Many seek answers, but that's not what they need most. It is better that our questions lead us to God without answers than that we find answers without God. As David says in Psalm 23:4,

Even though I walk through the valley of the shadow of death,
>   I will fear no evil,
> for *you* are with me.

True peace isn't found in the absence of pain (or even the answers to pain); true peace is found in the presence of God. In Scripture, peace always comes from a *who*, not merely a *why*.

I said above that suffering doesn't necessarily give you better words to say, but it does make you more generous with your tears. It gives unique perspective. Salvadoran Archbishop Oscar Romero is often quoted as having said, "There are many things that can only be seen through eyes that have cried." This is doubly true for the pastor. Suffering is difficult but necessary. More than leading people to *answers*, we want to remind sufferers that they have *access* to a great Comforter. Our pain is meant to lead us to a Person.

As I have helped my congregation, God has taught me four lessons on shepherding them through the valley of the shadow of death.

1. Warn Them That Affliction Lies Ahead

My aim here is not to produce sadness but sobriety. The biggest hindrance to leading a church through suffering isn't ignorance about steps to take but a lack of sobriety about suffering in general.

In January 2015, we sat in a living room with about thirty people who would be the founding members of Cornerstone Church. In hopes of instilling our vision into them, we worked through our core values (standard practice for church planters). I had the task of teaching about longevity. I focused on the unknowable future, a future that would certainly include affliction. If we desired to plant deep roots and grow old together, then that meant we would experience a lot of pain together. I pointed out that we would eventually bury people present in that room. It would come sooner than we thought and more often than we'd like. We needed to be prepared.

You can imagine how that went over in a room full of twenty- and thirty-somethings. Afterward, several friends told me how morbid I had been, how I had sucked all the life and energy out of the room. Everyone was feeling good about this church plant thing until I came in with all my death talk. And I thought, *Maybe they're right. We should be celebrating at a time like this. Maybe I was too morbid.* From that point on, I shied away from talking about death. But I was a coward. I was concerned about everyone's feelings, so I disregarded a certainty that lies in every person's future.

I look back at that meeting and wish I knew then what I do now. I should have let that God-given foresight set the agenda for our church, rather than planning to respond to future pain with answers. The difficulty is that if you talk about pain and suffering while people are enjoying prosperity or are full of hope for the future, you will have to push through the criticism. Your words won't be welcomed or showered with applause. That's because pain and suffering make for an uncomfortable conversation. You'll have to remind yourself that you're not being pessimistic—that you're in good company. Ecclesiastes 7:1–4 teaches us to define what's good in this life not by looking to our feelings but by looking to our future—namely, that everyone of us faces death and suffering.

Not everyone will have to wrestle with the temptations that go along with prosperity in this life. Not everyone will get the job of their dreams and have to fight with idolatry that can come with blessing. But absolutely everyone will wrestle with adversity.

We tend to think of two different groups when we read in Romans 12:15, "Rejoice with those who rejoice, weep with those who weep." But is it possible for the same person to rejoice and weep in the same situation? I can rejoice in God's goodness while simultaneously being sad at the prospect of loss or misfortune. The two responses aren't mutually exclusive. That's because both are common experiences for God's people.

When you plan your preaching calendar, factor in time to deal with pain and suffering. Don't wait for tough times to come. If you wait, you've already lost a valuable ministry opportunity. It's hard to be objective in times of stress.

Sobriety needs to be cultivated and maintained. Plan your preaching calendar with this perspective in mind. Don't even wait until it comes up in a text, but plan to preach texts that force believers to face hard realities. And when you go there, *go there!* The only thing worse than real pain is false hope, so give your people a firm place to stand. Be aware that sometimes you may need help from outside the church, especially in the field of counseling.

The way to shepherd a church through a season of suffering is by shepherding them before it arrives. If you prepare for a tornado the moment you see the funnel cloud, you're too late. Tornadoes of suffering are coming, more often than you like and sooner than you think. Prepare yourself and your congregation now.

2. Establish the Church as a Place of Refuge

Suffering is compounded when endured in silence. Whenever pain comes, people turn somewhere to cope. As a pastor, you want the church to be that place. When your members need encouragement and prayer, the church should be a refuge in God. Yet, the church won't automatically be that refuge. Painful times reveal fears, doubts, anger, hidden sins, and much else, and people need to know they can be real about their feelings. They need to have room to both rejoice and mourn. It is up to you to make sure your church is established as a place of honesty and transparency.

Right or wrong, members often measure their spirituality by the example of their pastor. So you must lead out in vulnerability and transparency. Let your people know you're human. Far from losing credibility in their eyes, it allows them to see that they aren't crazy for feeling depressed, angry, bitter, or even alone in doubting God's goodness. The psalmists model this dynamic well for us. And where would we be without knowing of Jesus's agony in Gethsemane, his cries of abandonment from the cross, and the reassurance that he sympathizes with our weakness?

3. Build a Team

Helping people battle with pain or carrying the weight of their suffering alone equals spiritual suicide for a pastor. Don't do it alone. No matter where you stand on the need for a plurality of elders/

pastors, from experience I can tell you how vital sharing the load is to the life of the church, and how crucial it'll be in dark places. Our church began with four pastors, and in God's kind providence, that is likely one of the reasons our church exists today. The day before our first outreach, I remember sitting in my living room crying with fellow pastors Richard, Trip, and Moe, after depression had taken a toll on my marriage. This shared leadership gave me freedom to reconcile with my wife while other brothers handled the load of preaching and leading. It reminded me that though I'm a shepherd, I'm still one of the sheep. I'm a church member who needs care, rest, and relief.

My spiritual brothers' willingness to carry the load saved my life. When I was unable to deal with my own family's suffering, much less the church's, these men carried the congregation. They were God's gift to our church. In hindsight, I wish I had trusted them even more, enough to really step back. I wish I'd surrendered all decision-making power during those first months. I couldn't see clearly, and I should have let them decide my workload, my time off, and what I could handle instead of trying to be Superman. I would've been much healthier. Our church would have been healthier.

Get others you know well and who know you well to help you carry this weight. Dealing with your own suffering is soul crushing. Dealing with suffering vicariously and continually is too much for one person to bear.

4. Know That Honest Praying Is as Important as Honest Preaching

E. M. Bounds wrote: "Talking to men for God is a great thing, but talking to God for men is greater still. He will never talk well and with real success to men for God who has not learned well how to talk to God for men."[1]

We've all been a part of churches where prayer is present but not really purposeful or potent. Prayer in church often feels like

---

1. E. M. Bounds, *Power through Prayer* (Norcross, GA: Trinity Press, 2012), chap. 4.

prayer before a meal—it's obligatory, and everyone respects your decision to do it, but no one really puts much into it. Prayer is reduced to the best way to transition from one activity to the next. As I think of seminary, I remember praying at the start and ending of class, but I don't recall a professor pausing to pray amid a heated debate.

Seminary taught me the mechanics of prayer, and it sounded quite simple: Reverence before request, and presence before provision. But when you awake in the morning with a thousand things on your mind, and feelings of doubt and discouragement assault you, those principles of prayer have to become more than catchy phrases. Seminary can teach you scriptural knowledge and theology, but those essentials alone do not necessarily produce spiritual growth.

These recent years have sobered me. I had built terrible habits for personal prayer. I'd pray, routinely confess sin, and ask God for help, but from an emotional standpoint, my prayer life was shallow. Prior to my brother's passing and my church's suffering, I had lived as if I didn't really need God. I lived as if I could handle my cares and the church's cares on my own. After my brother died, I was angry with God. It was a deep, abiding anger that wasn't resolved in a day, a week, or a month. It shaped all of 2015 for me.

I couldn't prepare to preach without first pouring out all my emotions to God. Otherwise my sermons would be cold and disconnected—and they *were* for a while. Once being raw before God became a habit, I realized my prayer life should have looked this way all along. I now realize that before that season I didn't know what I was doing in prayer.

You will vicariously feel your congregation's pain, and you must learn to take those feelings to God. You'll never bear the weight of the church without a place to offload it. It will crush you. You'll want to give up. And if you don't give the stress to God, you'll likely take it out on others. Giving God your burdens will help you encourage the congregation. It frees you up to do what God has called you to, regardless of the season, and that's preach his Word.

Be Prepared for the Hard Road

The journey down the road of suffering is long and the burden is heavy. They are longer and heavier when you're responsible for walking the road alongside others. The road is longest and the burden heaviest when you're limping alongside others while dealing with your own affliction.

You must be prepared. But if by *prepared* you think I mean the way a dentist preps a mouth for a filling—numbing the gums and nerves to erase any sense of pain—then you've misunderstood me. There is no way to avoid the sting of death. Such preparation won't keep you from hurting.

My hope is for you to be prepared in a fashion consistent with Jesus's words to Peter in Luke 22:31–32: "Simon, Simon, behold, Satan demanded to have you, that he might sift you like wheat, but I have prayed for you that your faith may not fail. And when you have turned again, strengthen your brothers." Even though the pain is real, I pray it won't keep you from the Lord but will cause you to run to him. I pray that God will sustain and strengthen the faith that connected you to Jesus in the first place. I pray that you will be strengthened so you may, in turn, strengthen your brothers and sisters.

9

When to Accept a Call
or Leave My Church

Harry L. Reeder

The pastor was in his third year of ministry when the call came. But this call was different. Other calls had come and were easily set aside, but this one came from denominational leaders and therefore intensified the question of how he should respond.

The question presented a dilemma: His current ministry was going awfully well. In two years, the Lord had pulled the church back from the cliff of extinction. It had been slated to be closed and the property sold. But the church came back to life with strong membership growth. Initially, this revitalization ministry was overwhelming in its challenges, but by the grace of God it became exhilarating in light of dynamic spiritual and statistical growth. More than 50 percent of the growth consisted of new believers. A remarkable demographic profile reflecting the ethnic diversity of the community had emerged. Now the church was known as a multiethnic congregation that enjoyed a unified, gospel-saturated culture. Yet, with all these reasons to stay, the pastor was being called by denominational leaders to serve elsewhere.

In a second scenario, the call came on a beautiful January day when the pastor was playing golf on a stunning Miami course. The pastor was pretty certain in that moment he was right where God had called him! So, was this call sent by the Lord to reposition him in another ministry? Was it a call from the Lord designed to reaffirm his present ministry? Or was it merely a distraction to divert his focus from his true calling?

To make matters more confusing, the pastor had just received a phone call from one supportive member of his present church that included these disorienting words: "Pastor, I think you should know there are some elders along with some influential members who are having secret meetings to discuss the development and implementation of an exit plan for you, including a departure package."

These very different scenarios provide two illustrations of multiple dilemmas a pastor may face in his calling to serve a local church. Each raises an important question: Is there a biblically defined way for pastors to effectively process various calls in order to discern God's will?

Should I Go? Should I Stay?

This issue must first be framed biblically while praying for the answer to be saturated with wisdom from above. Deciding whether to leave your present ministry for another place of service is not as simple as it may seem. The default answer of many ministers seems to be, "Things are going badly where I am, and there is a call before me to something that appears better. This must be from the Lord." Or, "Things are going great, so this call to go somewhere else must be a distraction to reject."

The above scenarios are more than two hypothetical illustrations. They are real-life situations that played out in my ministry. After extensive prayer and a thoughtful process, I ultimately left a "successful and exhilarating ministry," then later in life turned down a call that would have delivered me from what seemed to be a precarious situation. Why and how did I make these counterintuitive decisions? For the moment, let's forget each decision and focus on the process I used to reach a decision. To do this, we must begin with the concept of calling as developed in Scripture—calling to Christ for salvation, then calling to serve Christ in ministry vocation and location.

A Twofold Call

Just as God's work of salvation includes two calls—the external call of the proclaimed gospel and the internal effectual call of the Spirit—so too there is a similar twofold dynamic by which God calls men to ministry. If God has gifted a man to serve as a pastor or teaching elder, there will be a sense of that call internally by the Holy Spirit. God will also affirm that call externally through his church—reaffirming, refining, and directing his sense of calling.

It is crucial that men who believe they are called to ministry internally by the Spirit willingly submit to the leadership and fellowship of a local church so an internal call may be confirmed by an external call. If a church is exhorting men to embrace gospel ministry by external calling, it's equally important that the church inquire whether those inclined toward ministry have a true sense of internal calling. This is most notably articulated by the words of Paul—the same Paul called externally to ministry by the Lord on the Damascus road, the same Paul who was externally set apart for ministry with Barnabas by the church at Antioch. Paul wrote, "Woe to me if I do not preach the gospel" (1 Cor. 9:16). Not only was there a Spirit-inspired external call through the church to Paul; there was also a powerful internal calling that was so significant, he pronounced a malediction upon himself if he neglected, abandoned, or ignored the call.

Historically, evangelicals have not ordained men to ministry without a stated call from a local church. Ordination never precedes an external calling to a specific ministry by a local congregation and a willing submission to receive that call by the candidate.

Ten Lines of Guidance

Below are ten convictions or suggestions I have found helpful in processing various calls to ministry over the past forty-plus years. I believe they summarize answers to my ever-present prayer, "Lord give me wisdom from above."

Each time I have worked through a ministry call, I've never labored under the notion that I had to get the decision just right. My conviction has been that I have to get the process right with the motivation to glorify God and enjoy him forever, even as I've sought to discern his will in the ministry.

1. *The internal call is necessary to confirm the external call.* If there is no internal call, then you must dismiss any and all external calls. In other words, if the Lord is calling you by his Spirit through his church, he will bear witness to that call in your heart. This doesn't mean an internal call will immediately be present when the external call arrives. Sometimes it develops in the process of prayerfully addressing an external call. Nor does this mean that when one is called internally, no concerns will surface following an external call. I have served three churches, and each one extended an external call. In each, the internal call was made obvious by the Holy Spirit. Yet each process of ascertaining God's internal leading differed in degrees of time, intensity, and assurance.

2. *The external call is necessary to confirm an authentic internal call.* If there is an internal call to a specific ministry, it will ultimately be confirmed by an external call as the Spirit leads the church in concert with what he is leading the minister to be and do. If there is no external call, one should assume he has mistaken what he thinks to be an internal call—at least for the moment.

3. *Calling from God is not only to a vocation but also to a location and a population.* "Shepherd the flock of God that is among you," Peter wrote (1 Pet. 5:2). In pastoral ministry you are called not only to a role but also to a place. You are going not simply to a job—to preach sermons, enact leadership vision, or shep-

herd programs. You are being called to a people who make up the congregation.

4. *There is inseparable interdependence and dynamic interplay between the internal and external callings to ministry.* In vocational ministry, you may be called away from one location and population to another. Your internal calling away from one ministry sometimes precedes the external call as part of the Lord's preparing you for your next ministry. At other times, the reverse may be true. You may be called to another location in ministry with an external call before you are internally called away from your existing location.

5. *Be slow to let an external call consume your prayers or divert your current ministry focus.* This is merely a suggestion I embraced after a mentor offered it to me. Ministers who are being sought by other churches can end up spending much of their time praying about whether they should leave for another place. In my experience early in ministry, it seemed I was continually fielding requests to pray about the possibility of going to other locations. I sensed I was praying too often about leaving my present ministry. So I sought advice from a trusted mentor. He advised me never to consider or pray about another ministry opportunity unless those offering it returned to renew the call after I had said no three times. If they returned a fourth time, I'd pray about whether God was leading me from my present place of service to another.

6. *Stay the course, finish the race.* Adversity in your present ministry should never be the determining factor as to whether the Lord is calling you to leave for another ministry. Nor should the mistaken notion that another ministry will be without adversity.

Many pastors, because of an understandable desire to escape difficulty, leave a ministry too soon. Most church turnarounds require at least three to five years of thoughtful, consistent, faithful ministry, but many pastors leave within the first eighteen to thirty months. Certainly God is sovereign and uses these decisions, but had the pastors stayed the course a few months longer, perhaps their churches would have turned around.

7. *Present blessing is not a reason to dismiss an external call to another ministry location.* This is the inverse of the last suggestion. I was engaged in one ministry with significant opposition, and an opportunity to leave arose. Yet I sensed I should stay and see the present ministry to completion. Over the next year, significant opposition gave way to significant blessing. The Lord is still using that congregation to faithfully proclaim the gospel. In another place, a challenging ministry opportunity was offered while the current ministry was prospering in the Lord. Although I faced significant personal struggles as I worked through the decision, it became obvious I shouldn't stay simply because the Lord was blessing.

This same dynamic is the method by which God calls men to pastoral ministry in general, and to a church in particular. Arguably, I was close to idolatry when the blessings of the Lord in ministry had nearly become more important to me than the Lord's will. I was aware the Lord could quickly make those blessings a curse if my idolizing of ministry blessings replaced humble availability for a new ministry direction. In that case, I moved to the next ministry, and the Lord made it abundantly clear it was the right thing to do, even though there was much to enjoy where I was already serving, and the new location promised difficulties.

8. *Don't be a hireling.* Knowing my own weaknesses as well as the call of my life verse—"Seek first the kingdom of God and his righteousness, and all these things will be added to you" (Matt. 6:33)—I have instituted two practices to avoid being a hireling and, therefore, avoid the temptation to make ministry decisions based on salary.

These practices are born out of two convictions. First, if the Lord calls me somewhere, he will use his people to support me properly when and however they are able. If he has called me and they do not properly support me, he is perfectly capable of sustaining me. Remember, God used ravens to support his prophet Elijah. He can likewise encourage me and convict those who aren't doing what God has called them to do. The second conviction is overriding. I am aware of my own tendencies to be influenced by prestige and salary packages. Therefore, to flee temptation, I have embraced the following two lifelong commitments related to the pastor's support package.

First, I never talk about my salary package with church leadership. I recognize and affirm their right and responsibility to ask about our needs, and therefore they are free to speak with my wife, Cindy, who knows more about our financial circumstances than I do. This includes never talking about salary increases. I simply trust the responsible parties to do what is right and support me in a manner that appropriately fits the lifestyle of our congregation.

Second, when I move from one ministry to another, the first-year salary package can never exceed the salary I was receiving in the previous ministry. My convictions on this issue have led to some interesting conversations in the three churches I have served. In one situation, the chairman of the search committee said, "Well, we have talked about everything but your salary package. What do you need?" I said, "This one is easy. Go find out what I was paid last year in my ministry (since I don't know) and pay me something less than that. As for the next year, talk with Cindy."

9. *Adopt models, mentors, and motivators.* I believe every minister needs to adopt three to five models from history or the Bible as examples to follow in ministry development. Additionally, I believe that every pastor needs three to five mentors for counsel, direction, and ministry coaching. A pastor also needs three to five motivators (a band of brothers) or ministry peers with whom he meets regularly for encouragement, accountability, and prayer. While it's impossible to converse with your bygone models (as they are with the Lord), it is possible and mandatory, when considering a call away from one ministry to another, that you spend time with your mentors and motivators.

Choose your mentors and motivators carefully, because we

become like our teachers. Share with them the dynamics and facts of your situations, listen to their input, and prayerfully process their observations. It's amazing what others on the outside can see about you, your ministry, your tendencies. They are often able to give an accurate assessment of ministry opportunities offered you. Mentors and motivators are not infallible but should be honored and used. Remember, "there is wisdom in many counselors" (cf. Prov. 11:14), but make sure you have chosen wise counselors as mentors and motivators.

10. *Seek family wisdom.* Fully use your family at the appropriate time and in the appropriate way. You should first discuss the situation with your wife. What does she see in the dynamics of leaving the present ministry? What does she think about the possibilities of a future ministry? Give her time to pray and process her thoughts as you also bathe the matter with prayer. In each of the churches I've served, Cindy and I took a three-day retreat for prayer and fasting before arriving at a final decision. The retreat had been preceded by numerous conversations.

Finally, it is my conviction that when we use a God-glorifying, Spirit-filled, biblically framed, Christ-honoring process, the Lord will grant us a sense of peace in our final decision. The decision may still include concerns. The same Paul who said "be anxious for nothing" (Phil. 4:6) also confessed that he had "anxiety for all the churches" (2 Cor. 11:28).

God will give you peace as you make decisions that exalt Christ, seek the well-being of the body of Christ, and rest in the power of the Spirit to minister the gospel of Christ for the preeminence of Christ.

The words of the apostle give us confidence:

I am sure of this, that he who began a good work in you will bring it to completion at the day of Jesus Christ. (Phil. 1:6)

He who calls you is faithful; he will surely do it. (1 Thess. 5:24)

10

How to Handle Conflict

Jay Thomas

There are essentially two kinds of pastors: those who know that local church ministry involves frequent conflict, and those who are about to learn this painful truth. You might be a man about to cross the threshold into your first pastoral post. If so, here's a warning: the church you are about to serve will have conflict. But don't run away! Conflict is an opportunity, not a deal-breaker.

Because we minister in a fallen world, every church has conflict. Most of the New Testament letters were written to embattled churches. Your faithful, godly, biblical ministry will not bleach your church of imperfection, but it will set a course for maturation, one that is less conflicted every year, one that is more and more useful to God as it embodies the gospel. God has taught me many lessons in my own pastoral journey through the fires of church conflict.

What Is Conflict?
Let's begin with definitions. I am going to focus on relational conflict between believers within the church, not conflict between

God's people and the unbelieving world, which falls more into the category of persecution.

Also, I want to narrow the field to four types of conflict:

1. Between church members
2. Between the congregation and church leaders
3. Between the congregation and its lead pastor
4. Between church leaders

And here are three important presuppositions: (1) conflict must be dealt with; (2) only the power of the gospel can heal it; and (3) Christ-centered love, not the absence of conflict, is the final goal.

1. Conflict between Church Members

Sin will continue to indwell Christians until Jesus returns. It doesn't take long to become aware of this reality. As you counsel marrieds, hold member meetings, overhear conversations, and take the spiritual pulse of the church, you will learn of broken relationships all around.

Some issues will be organizational—the direction of the church, off-putting ministry decisions, people rubbing each other the wrong way while serving together. Other issues will be personal. In one situation I faced, two families had raw feelings because one of the fathers owned a business that employed a child in the other family. For various reasons, the child was released from employment during a particularly sensitive time. Imagine the stress this put on those relationships. Unfortunately, both families were in the same life group at church.

The fundamental issue in all conflict is the heart. Whether the conflict seems more objective, like a ministry decision, or more subjective, like personal offenses, it all stems from hearts not totally satisfied in and yielded to Christ. This is probably the most important truth to raise when dealing with conflict. Conflict arises out of hearts that have not fully embraced the glories of the gospel.

How do you begin to deal with these situations? Paul provides a helpful example. Conflict and disunity appear throughout the Bible.

First Corinthians and Philippians address disharmony and conflict directly. Paul uses slightly different approaches, but he aims in both letters to show how the gospel draws Christians back to unity in Christ. (I'll comment on Philippians a bit later, on p. 97.) In 1 Corinthians 1:1–4, Paul lays down a theological vision of Christ crucified. This cross-centered vision goes against the grain of the Greco-Roman worldview, which was destroying relationships and attitudes within the Corinthian church. Those Christians were failing to live according to the gospel because their self-oriented hearts embraced self-centered narratives rather than the true story of a crucified King. Paul goes straight to the heart. The glorious exposition of Christ-defined love in chapter 13, the hinge of the letter, reveals the full expression of a church with Jesus at its center.

The first way we deal with conflict is to preach the gospel. That means more than just your pulpit work, but it is not less than that weekly practice. This is why expository preaching is so valuable: as you preach the Word, you inevitably preach the gospel , and you quickly realize the Bible is full of conflict-healing truths. The Bible addresses pride, self-righteousness, snobbishness, idolatry, self-preservation, and other sins often at the root of conflict. The goal is not mere neutrality but love. You will be amazed and encouraged as the Holy Spirit uses God's Word to convict people of their roles in causing discord and to move them toward maturity, replacing resentment with the love of Christ.

This means you have to do the hard work of confronting conflict when you see it, hear of it, or sense it within the church. Many pastors hold good and biblical principles about how conflict is resolved, but they don't want to get dirty in the process. The process of confrontation is dirty, but this is part of your call as a shepherd. As in conversion, God must perform a miracle to awaken a sinful heart in conflict resolution. The Word faithfully preached is the best place to start.

2. Conflict between the Congregation and Church Leaders

Whether you serve on a multi-staff team or you are a solo pastor surrounded by lay leaders, you will experience tension between the congregation and the leadership. Various occasions will trigger this type of conflict, but it tends to come in discernible patterns.

My church has gone through many changes since I arrived more than six years ago. I serve on a multi-staff team, but we are also elder-led and committed to a plurality of leaders in setting the church's vision and direction. A few "big" decisions have disappointed some of our people, even though they were made for the health of our body. These "big" decisions were more cultural than doctrinal, but it is often said that culture eats strategy for breakfast. This is true.

There will be moments when your leadership favors major shifts in church culture and ethos. These changes will create tension between the congregation and the leadership team. Change your service structure, preach differently, shift the leadership structure, hire new staffers, let older leaders go, or start a capital campaign—all are often necessary and vital moves that lead the church toward gospel health, but they are also ecosystems for tension. Don't be discouraged. Still, these tensions must be addressed with the gospel and embodied in love.

As with conflict between members, the gospel provides the method for dealing with conflict between the congregation and its leaders. You may become aware of such conflict through comments, notes, emails, or even gossip. Once you are aware of this kind of a conflict, gather key leaders and begin to pray and talk about shepherding your people. Here are some steps to consider:

1. *Meet with people who seem to be leading the opposition.* First, hear them out. If possible, get the back story. If you can win them with pastoral love and gospel truth, then these leaders may turn and guide others back to a place of trust and love.

2. *Hold a town hall meeting to discuss the issues.* My church just finished the teaching phase of a capital campaign. Leaders felt that we honored the Lord in how we conceived of and executed this phase. Of course, there were many things we could have done better, but hopefully we were biblically motivated and Spirit-led. This was, however, a massive culture shift. It caused travail among some people.

A significant majority of our church favored the campaign and its related building project, but it was important to allow members to ask questions and express concerns in a public forum. We could have just moved on without their input, but we wanted to shepherd the people and win them to the mission of our church.

3. *If leaders have contributed to conflict, they must confess it, repent of it, seek forgiveness, and ask God to use the occasion to help them mature as leaders.* Humility, teachableness, and willingness to admit sin and mistakes are massive assets in quelling conflict in the moment and mitigating it in the long run. Humble, godly leadership creates a church culture of trust and love.

Whether it is one-on-one or in group settings, when people see you pursue them as brothers and sisters in Christ and not as personal supporters or troublemakers, trust grows. To the degree your leadership reflects humble shepherding, your church will grow to trust its leaders and focus more on mission and less on protecting its traditional intra-church culture. Love will replace skepticism, mistrust, and resentment.

3. Conflict between the Congregation and Its Lead Pastor

Unfortunately, there will be seasons in which conflict will focus on you. Of course, you don't have to be a lead pastor for this to happen, or even a staff pastor. Still, you must keep to the same method: address it directly, "gospel it," and work toward Christlike love.

Philippians comes to mind here. Conflict seems to have arisen between two women in the church, Euodia and Syntyche (Phil. 4:2). Paul does not seem to be defending himself in this matter, as in 1 and 2 Corinthians. However, the theology he uses to define unity is important in how we respond to conflict. In Philippians 2:1–11, Paul paints a beautiful picture of Jesus pouring himself out in humility— in the incarnation and on the cross—out of obedience to the Father and love for his people, resulting in his glory and universal praise. When leaders are accused, maligned, even rejected, this is a golden truth to which they may cling. This is a pertinent truth even if you realize your sin, idolatry, or self-centered ambitions have contributed to the conflict and hurt others.

You must do the difficult but necessary work of meeting with people with whom you are experiencing conflict. Talk about behaviors, but as soon as possible, get to the heart. Listen well. Be prepared for the process to take time. Often it is helpful to bring along another leader as both a witness and a source of objective wisdom. Consult with others in your church and outside it, seeking to learn where you may have contributed to the problem—not for vindication but for repentance. In 2 Corinthians 11–12, Paul defends himself, but he does so by commending.

Conflict that focuses on you is perhaps the most challenging, but it can also be the most fruitful. It forces you to cling to Christ, reinforces that your value and identity are found in Christ instead of human approval, challenges you to examine your own shortcomings, and allows you to shepherd even when the sheep are biting. These circumstances, though painful, will contribute to your credibility if handled well. Don't run from people who have it out for you. Instead, try to run *to* them. You may not win all of them. Some don't want to be won. You will win some, and those who watch will grow in trusting you and in their appreciation of the gospel as they see its effects in you.

4. Conflict between Church Leaders

Though I am addressing conflict between church leaders last, it is perhaps the most important point. How the leaders do life with each other shapes the entire church. It is sometimes said that the team you are on is more important than the team you lead.

Leaders must apply the gospel method with utmost rigor and passion. As long as you keep short accounts, conflict among the leaders will be rare, shallow, and even leveraged into growth.

Think of the leadership team as the parents of the church. Dads and moms will never be perfect, but they can grow daily by the power of grace, and that makes all the difference to the children.

You don't have to be a perfect leadership team; just grow together and seek Jesus together. And when inevitable conflict arises, deal with it quickly, with the gospel, and with the goal of godly love. Leadership teams I have seen mired in toxicity are those that do not allow the gospel of grace to grip the culture. Gifted and Jesus-loving people can sink into disunity if they do not glory in the gospel together and apply its security and forgiveness to their own relationships. Disunity is an ugly sight. But the sight of a leadership growing by grace, in good times and challenging times, is simply beautiful.

Merely a Crash Course

This has been a brief crash course on conflict. It does not deal with the nuances and gray areas. What about conflict that runs so deep, a third party must get involved? What if someone has mental-health issues or such deep heart issues that professional counseling and other intense mechanisms need to be put in place? What if the conflict persists beyond your best efforts, and when might that signal that it is time to leave?

All are important questions, and many pastors will face them. I believe if you stick to the three-pronged approach of addressing conflict, using the power and truth of the gospel to address it, and aiming for the full goal of love, when you face an unusually potent level of conflict, the way forward will be more clear, and there will be a lot less collateral damage to your soul, the church, and the kingdom.

Pastors, persevere! The conflict you may be facing right now is under God's control. Rest in the gospel, proclaim the gospel, and live out the effects of the gospel. At least, you can be at peace when conflict inevitably erupts.

11

The Need to Fight for My Relationship with God

Vermon Pierre

It's a distinct and disconcerting feeling. It comes over you when you have to preach a sermon on a Sunday after you have struggled over the past week, or perhaps the past couple of weeks, in your own relationship with God. It's difficult to put into words. The closest analogy I can think of is the morning I came out of the shower but found no towel waiting. This left me having to cover myself with a washcloth while I scurried to the towel closet, hoping no one was awake yet.

There you are, about to preach the Word of God. The very Word of God! But rather than feeling charged and ready, you feel raw and naked. You feel what you are about to do will fall flat, because *you* have felt flat for several weeks. You fight back a gnawing fear that in the next forty minutes, you will be exposed as a fraud.

Honesty. Genuineness. Authenticity. These aren't optional values for the pastor. Your whole persona, your major "selling point," is that you are "real" with people. No pastor wants to be known as fake. Add to that the expectation that your preaching will be gospel-centered, Jesus-focused, Holy Ghost–fired every single Sunday. And not just on Sunday morning. Whether you are teaching a Sunday school class, leading a small group, or counseling, you're expected to speak wise, heart-piercing, soul-convicting words that will capture attention and change hearts.

Truth is, those weekly expectations don't always fully match the current state of your own soul. Pastors are always "real," in the sense that they are real *Christians*, and thus real sinners in the midst of their sanctification. Real Christians will really struggle at times to have a vibrant relationship with God.

The War Within

I felt this struggle keenly nearly four years ago. Racially charged incidents between minorities and law enforcement in Ferguson, Missouri, and in New York City, with Eric Garner, had recently unfolded. I had strong feelings about these and similar incidents, but I struggled to find space to fully explore them. I was tired from arguing about it on social media and frustrated that so many disagreements were marked by harsh words and sarcasm instead of grace and empathy. For many weeks, I felt tired and drained. I ground through my days, trying my best to fulfill my ministerial duties but feeling distant from others and from God.

Images used to describe the Christian life—how it is like a battle (Eph. 6:10–20; 2 Tim. 2:3–4) or a long race (1 Cor. 9:24–27; Heb. 12:1–2)—are not arbitrary or exaggerated. A relationship with God *is* hard, and it *will* take hard work to maintain it.

It's *hard* because we are living in a sinful world, still dealing with sin that clings to us (Heb. 12:1). This makes a relationship with the Lord feel like running barefoot on a sandy beach. You can run fairly fast. But in the running you are constantly aware of the sand, how it stubbornly clings to your legs and feet and accumulates between your toes. You are aware of how it takes extra effort to keep a steady pace. You are tempted to slow down, even stop, in especially difficult parts of the beach during especially hot parts of the day.

It's hard *work* because building a healthy walk with God defies a quick, drive-through-window kind of relationship. It requires regular, persistent prayer. It requires prolonged meditation on the Scriptures. This demand does not fit well with my life today. I have a laptop that fires up instantly and a smartphone that responds to my thumbprint activation before I can blink. All around me is speed, efficiency, immediacy. Every week is full and busy, and on many days I think, *Well, of course I need to read the Bible and pray. I'm a pastor, and that's the most basic job requirement. But I only have five minutes to do this. Let's see if I can get by with five minutes of Bible reading and prayer.* Of course, this never works. It is impossible to build a mature relationship by spending five minutes with a person every day.

But, let's say you consistently read your Bible and pray. It's still hard work, especially as you deal with doubts, fears, disappointments, and challenges that arise constantly. You can do all the right things externally yet still feel like God is encased in multiple layers of hard ice while you try to break through with a butter knife.

The Battle Belongs to the Lord

How do you avoid giving up? How do you keep going? How do you keep fighting for your relationship with God? The main way you persevere at any pursuit in life, even when the going gets difficult, is to be sufficiently motivated to keep doing it. Fortunately, the Lord has from the beginning taken it upon himself to motivate his people to remain in relationship with him. How? By constantly reminding them of the kind of God he is and all he has done to establish and maintain the relationship.

Remembering God and His Works

In Exodus 12, the Israelites were commanded to participate annually in the Passover as a regular remembrance of how the Lord judged the Egyptians and spared his people.

In Joshua 4, the Israelites were commanded to set up twelve stones at Gilgal after crossing the Jordan River. This was to be a regular reminder of their covenant relationship with a mighty, awesome God, one who had brought them safely through the river and the sea.

Psalms is a hymnal for God's people. And this hymnal is full of reminders of who God is and what he has done (Pss. 44:1–4; 81:10; 84:11–12; 91:1–2; 103:1, 8; 125:1–2). Indeed, the Psalter directly instructs us to remember and reflect on the Lord and how he works for his people (Ps. 34:8; 77:11; 111:2).

These passages encourage us to see that the Lord is a saving, redeeming, promise-keeping God. They are among the clearest snapshots of what a relationship with the Lord is like; they illustrate how God is always pursuing his people.

Examples from Scripture may be multiplied, of course. These passages were written for the benefit of God's people now as then. Like ancient Israel, God's people today quickly forget the benefits of the Lord. This is why prayerful, meditative reading of key Bible passages is an immediately helpful way to revive our hearts.

Do This in Remembrance of Me

The capstone biblical example and most concrete way the Lord points us to himself is through the Lord's Supper. The Lord's Supper regularly reminds us that we relate to a God who gave himself for us in Jesus Christ so that we might have an eternally blessed relationship with him.

Indeed, the way we practice the Supper helps us see that this forever relationship with God is not built on a mere intellectual rehearsal of theological propositions. Through the bread and cup God builds "muscle memory" within us, giving us a renewed sense of what a relationship with him truly "feels" like.

In Jesus, God's saving, redeeming, and promise keeping are on full display. The more we see and remember the ways the Lord has saved us and is sanctifying us through the work of Jesus, the more we will desire to pursue him and work toward a mature relationship with him.

Two Other Vital Habits

Added fuel for godly living comes from two additional, vital means:

1. *Spending time with other godly believers.* I participate in a monthly prayer meeting, and it has been a massive help for my ministry. Praying with spiritually healthy believers allows you to, in a sense, be carried along on the wings of their supplications and helped in your own prayer life. This holds true during times of corporate prayer as well. The prayers of fellow believers in corporate worship of God are, not surprisingly, a helpful way to stir one's individual worship of God during the week.

Fellowship with other believers is also crucial. Warm hugs, loving words of truth, hopeful stories about God's ongoing work in lives, generous sharing of food and laughter—these experiences in fellowship with believers will strengthen your walk. Remember, you are not the only one in relationship with the Lord. The gathering of the many, the church, is woven into the Christian experience as a means by which we receive care and grow in our faith (1 Cor. 12:7, 27; Heb. 10:25).

2. *Leveraging everyday grace that God provides us in life and worship.* In addition to regular prayer and daily Bible reading, a number of regular practices can refresh us when we feel spiritually dry. For example:

- *Regular rhythms of rest.* While we do not practice the Sabbath in exactly the way it was observed in Old Testament times, its existence tells us that regular times of rest are vital for our relationship with the Lord.
- *Experiencing God's creation.* If the "heavens declare the glory of God" (Ps. 19:1), and God's "eternal power and divine nature" can be seen in the creation (Rom. 1:20), then it makes sense that time in the natural world can be a powerful way for the believer to experience God's beauty and goodness.
- *Singing with other believers.* Music has a unique ability to touch both our minds and our feelings. Singing words that focus on the gospel alongside other believers is a direct way to better understand ourselves in relation to God (Col. 3:16).

- *Serving others.* If it is true that God equips us to serve others, then humble service will always be a way we get a richer sense of God's presence in our lives (1 Pet. 4:10). One of the best ways to experience God's grace is to be a conduit of his mercy to others. Often the greatest joys we experience in the Lord come from time spent working for the good of others. This should not surprise us since through these acts we are modeling God's love for us in Christ.

- *Hearing God's Word preached and taught.* Pastors spend much time preaching and teaching God's Word to others. They also benefit from placing themselves under the preaching and teaching of others. We do well to lean more often on the gifts of preaching and teaching God has given other men in our church. If God works through people sitting and receiving biblical instruction from us, we should take opportunities to receive biblical instruction from other preachers and teachers.

The Ongoing Battle

We must fight for a relationship with God because it won't happen automatically, even among pastors. May we never presume to be right with the Lord because of anything we are doing as pastors. Rather, let's assume we need a fresh awakening of our hearts daily. Indeed, there are many enemies making war against us. There are many distractions, many challenges, many disappointments. All these factors and many more make the fight seem doubly hard.

Thankfully, the Lord has already fought hard for a relationship with us—to the point of death on a cross. And mercifully, he won! So seek the Lord today with the knowledge that he is already close by and ready to fill your heart full of faith, hope, and love.

> The LORD is near to all who call on him,
> to all who call on him in truth.
> He fulfills the desire of those who fear him;
> he also hears their cry and saves them. (Ps. 145:18–19)

12

The Time It Takes to Become a Shepherd

Dale Van Dyke

It would have been helpful if someone had explained to me that pastoring a congregation is much like dairy farming.

I grew up on a small, family-owned-and-operated dairy farm in West Michigan. In other words, I had an intimate relationship with sixty Holsteins and their young. I knew their names, unique markings, and quirks. We milked them twice a day, cared for them when they were sick, ran after them when they broke through the fence, bore the injustice of malicious kicks, and grieved their untimely deaths.

And we fed them. Twice a day. Every single day. If we weren't feeding them, we were planting/tilling/harvesting and storing feed for them. In return they gave us the daily gift of milk: a huge tank of frothing, creamy, white nectar.

A Secret Learned the Hard Way

Shepherding a congregation is a lot like that. It involves intimate knowledge, intense labor, occasional bruises, and constant feeding—

all to produce "much fruit" to the glory of the Father (John 15:8). But shepherding—whether it be flocks, flights, or folks—has a secret, indispensable ingredient. Trust. They won't let you into their space until they trust you.

I learned this lesson the hard way; actually, my city-slicker buddy did first. We were about ten years old, and he was fearful of the large beasts I cared for, so I decided to show him how safe they truly were. The cows were standing side by side in their stanchions, creating a sort of corridor underneath their bellies. My brother and I made a game of crawling the length of the barn through this hall of Holsteins. After watching us do it, my young friend tried it. I was shocked when the third cow down the row protested with a kick! She knew me and was comfortable with my presence. But she didn't know or trust this stranger (cf. John 10:5), and she let him know it.

I've seen good men suffer nasty bruises from the Lord's sheep because they moved forward without first gaining the essential element of trust. It is a non-negotiable necessity.

But the first-time pastor has a unique challenge: How do you gain the trust of your flock when you are new not only to the congregation but to the ministry itself? How do you instill confidence in them when you secretly share their questions concerning your abilities?

How to Build Trust

Here are four things I learned along the way:

1. Be Patient

Young pastors tend to be eager—eager to make a difference, zealous to see the church move forward. But shepherding, like farming, requires patience. The newly sown hayfield won't yield much the first year, the newborn calf won't produce anything for nearly two years, and the newly planted apple trees will take six to ten!

Trust isn't a Chia Pet—sprinkle a little water and watch the miracle. Trust takes time to grow. The best thing we can do is patiently provide good soil in which trust may take root. I think that's precisely why

Paul counsels young Timothy as he does in the classic "young pastor's text": "Let no one despise you for your youth, but set the believers an example in speech, in conduct, in love, in faith, in purity" (1 Tim. 4:12).

Timothy was in a tough spot. In stark contrast to our youth-venerating culture, Timothy was ministering in a culture that honored age and trusted experience. His "youth" (commentators suggest he was between thirty-five and forty) would have been a real obstacle in the congregation's eyes. You can almost see the raised eyebrows and hear the mutters in the corner of the foyer: "What was Paul thinking when he installed this timid *youngster* as shepherd of the church in an intensely pagan city like Ephesus? We need a man's man, a true leader!" Poor Timothy—he was shepherding a flock that hadn't called him and didn't trust him. His congregation seemed to believe he was in way over his head.

It's important to notice that Paul's instruction to this young pastor was not "Rebuke those who despise you for your youth." First Timothy 4:12 has often been read as a corrective for the congregation, but it's intended to be instructive for the young pastor. Paul was telling *Timothy* to do something, not telling the congregation to refrain from something. While Timothy couldn't change his age or the cultural presumptions of his congregation, he was called to help his flock overcome the obstacle of their distrust.

How? By setting an example for them in the whole of his life.

The authenticating mark of Timothy's ministerial authority was not to be found in his theological training or even his apostolic commissioning (which must have been a tempting card to play). Rather, the "signs and wonders" of his ministry were to be his speech, his conduct, his love, his faith, and his purity. Instead of despairing over his congregation's lack of appropriate respect, Timothy was to till the soil of trust by living an intentional, God-honoring, Spirit-empowered, Christ-exalting life before them. He was not powerless in the face of their cultural assumptions. There were particular, practical, and powerful things for him to do. A gospel-saturated life of faith, purity, and love were his tools for building trust.

Young pastors will save themselves and their congregation

much grief if they spend less time thinking about how they are being *received* and much more about how they are being *perceived*; what authenticating marks of gospel ministry are people seeing in your life? God's people need to see our calling in our demeanor, not our degree. By setting an example before your flock, you will be helping them overcome their fears and will gain their confidence.

This will take time. Use that time to manifest gospel humility.

2. Be Humble

In Paul's letters it is evident that one of the chief requirements of a servant of Christ is a humble, Christlike mind (Eph. 4:2; Phil. 2:3ff.). Young pastor, I beg you to put on humility (Col. 3:12). It is absolutely necessary in the horticulture of trust. And nearly nothing proves gospel humility like a teachable spirit in the face of criticism.

This is counterintuitive, but criticism early in your ministry is a great opportunity. It gives you a unique chance to show you are teachable, you realize this isn't all about you, you don't have it all figured out, and you can consider criticisms and complaints. It doesn't mean you will always agree with the critique. Over the years you will develop a sense of which concerns are worth listening to and which are best disregarded. Young pastors ought to do their best to listen broadly and humbly to concerns. Critical and angry sheep can still be right.

I distinctly remember having tea one fall afternoon with Miss Anne McQueen, a thoroughly Scottish, fearfully proper, elderly gentlewoman who had been a friend of theologian John Murray. She solemnly peered at me over her perfectly perched reading glasses, raised a cup of tea, and said in her blunt, beautiful brogue, "You seem to be a young man in a hurry."

It wasn't a compliment.

While most in the congregation appreciated my preaching, and said so, I knew there were concerns about my shepherding. Some left the church saying I was a poor pastor: "Not good at listening and counseling." As much as these concerns grieved me, I couldn't, in full honesty, say they were wrong. Honesty and humility about my weaknesses helped the congregation and allowed me to effectively, though imperfectly, minister to them.

A few years later I did something that deeply offended Miss McQueen. I heard about it through the grapevine. I failed to pray for her in the church service during a time of illness. She took full, self-righteous offense and stopped coming to worship services. I thought she was overreacting, and I didn't appreciate her voicing anger over my failures with other members without first talking to me. But I decided to humble myself. I wrote her a heartfelt letter in which I honestly admitted my oversight, acknowledged how it must have hurt, and asked for her forgiveness. I placed it in the mail in the confidence that I had honored the Lord. A few days later Miss McQueen invited me to her apartment and, with tears, thanked me for that letter and forgave me. She hadn't expected it but was profoundly blessed by it. A few years later I officiated at her funeral—honoring her request. I had earned her trust.

3. Minister in the Authority of God's Word

I love it that Paul's instruction to Timothy regarding his youth is bracketed by commands to minister the Word.

Command and teach these things. (1 Tim. 4:11)

Until I come, devote yourself to the public reading of Scripture, to exhortation, to teaching. (1 Tim. 4:13)

The wonderful thing about being a minister of the gospel is that the Word of God is everything that you, the inexperienced pastor, are not. You are young, untested, and not yet vested with the confidence of your congregation. What a joy to be able to bring to them the "very Word of God." It has intrinsic, unqualified, and unshakable authority, and you can assure your flock it will never, ever fail. Your ministry will be robed with divine authority as you forget yourself and joyfully proclaim God's own inerrant, infallible, and utterly sufficient Word.

You may be timid like Timothy. But God's Word is powerful

and dynamic. It's able to divide joints and marrow (Heb. 4:12). It is uniquely suited for teaching, reproof, correction, and training in righteousness (2 Tim. 3:16). As Herman Bavinck points out, Scripture is not merely "God-breathed" but "God-*breathing*."[1] Your lack of experience is no obstacle to God's divine power and purposes!

I remember well one of the most fearful pastoral visits I've ever made. Ron, a middle-aged man in our church, had been absent for several months. His long-suffering wife revealed he had been drinking hard and was constantly angry. Ron had been a full-bore, drinking-brawling pagan before being dramatically converted in his late twenties. In the few years he had been at our church, he was a full-bore Christian—delighting in worship and eagerly reading his Bible and Martyn Lloyd-Jones commentaries. But then some disappointments and spiritual apathy left him vulnerable to old, sinful patterns. He was caught in a besetting sin (Gal. 6:1), and we needed to go after him—but I was scared. Getting punched in the face was a distinct possibility.

In an attempt to encourage Ron toward rational behavior, I took my six-foot-ten-inch Dutch elder along, and the two of us sat down at this erring sheep's kitchen table. It didn't take long before Ron began angrily protesting our concerns and justifying his sinful behavior. But I had my Bible open on the table and, by the grace of God, I was able to answer every self-justifying argument and every blame-shifting ploy with a specific text from the Word of God. I would be turning to a passage God brought to mind while Ron was still fully engaged in his futile attempt to avoid conviction. He finally slammed his fist down on the table and with a curse got up and left the room. The elder and I sat looking at each other, wondering what the next moments would bring. Would he come back? Was he getting a baseball bat?

I'll never forget what happened next. Ron came to the table, collapsed into his chair, cradled his face in his folded arms on the table, and wept. Through his sobs he managed to say, "I know

---

1. Herman Bavinck, *Reformed Dogmatics*, ed. John Bolt, trans. John Vriend, vol. 1, *Prolegomena* (Grand Rapids, MI: Baker Academic, 2003), 385.

you're right. I'm so sorry. I can't argue with the Word. I need to repent." And he did. Full-bore. Three years later he died of cancer, in perfect peace.

The Word did all the work.

The Word is sufficient for the tasks for which you are utterly unprepared. As a young pastor I was often in "over my head." I faced counseling situations and crises that were completely beyond me. I had no grasp of the pain of parents losing a child, the devastation of a betrayed spouse, the shock of newly found cancer, the exhausting war with depression, or the challenges of a special-needs child. I had never experienced any of these things. How could I possibly have something meaningful and authentic to say? And yet, my congregation clearly expected that of me. One of the first calls members in crisis make is to the pastor—and they will expect you to give comfort.

I felt this tension forcibly one frigid night as I drove down a snow-blown city street at 1:00 a.m. A young mother of eight children had just died, at home, without warning. Sally had been the rock of her family and a vibrant part of our congregation. And now, an elder and I were driving through the freezing night to comfort her devastated family. The question swirled through my mind like the snowflakes in the headlights. Why did God allow this to happen? What was I going to say? How in the world do you comfort a family when their precious mother is lying dead on the floor? Who is sufficient for this task?

The Word of God is sufficient.

We went upstairs where her body lay, and several of the older children gathered around. We grieved, and then I read from John 11, and we laid hold of the reality of Jesus as the resurrection and the life. We proclaimed Sally's victory over death as we prayed, holding her deceased hands and, in faith, grasping Christ's living hands. Then we went downstairs and read from Psalm 121:

> From where does my help come?
> My help comes from the LORD,
>   who made heaven and earth. (vv. 1–2)

Behold, he who keeps Israel
>   will neither slumber nor sleep.

The LORD is your keeper. (vv. 4–5)

I, as a mere man, had nothing to offer that family. But as I opened the Word, our loving heavenly Father spoke to his dear, grieving children, and a living Christ assured those present-day Marys and Marthas of his triumph over death.

The Word is sufficient for you and your congregation. Teach it. Preach it. Pray it. Your congregation will come to trust you, unreservedly.

4. Be a Shepherd

Your congregation will come to trust you as their shepherd only as you act like one. I came out of seminary convinced that the church really needs men of conviction, men who aren't afraid to take a stand for the cause of the day. For graduation my mother gave me a framed, lovingly needle-stitched quote often (if mistakenly) attributed to Martin Luther. It reads:

> If I profess, with the loudest voice and the clearest exposition, every portion of the truth of God except precisely that little point which the world and the Devil are at that moment attacking, I am not confessing Christ, however boldly I may be professing Christianity. Where the battle rages the loyalty of the soldier is proved; and to be steady on all the battlefield besides is mere flight and disgrace to him if he flinches at that one point.[2]

I hung that quote on the wall of my new study and began my pastorate with the conviction that duty looked like theological rigor and a willingness to take a stand for contested doctrines.

It does.

But I soon began to realize being a pastor looks a lot more like

---

2. This powerful statement reflects Luther's ideas as expressed by a fictional character named Fritz in a historical novel by Elizabeth Rundle Charles, *Chronicles of the Schönberg-Cotta Family* (New York: Thomas Nelson, 1864), 276.

farming than fighting. Christ's command to Peter was "feed my sheep" (John 21:17). Wolves will appear (Acts 20:29), and the sheep will need to be protected with clear teaching and sincere warnings. But most days they just need to be cared for—fed with the gospel, washed with the water of the Word, and strengthened with gospel promises. The "battles" being fought in your congregation likely have little to do with cutting-edge theological issues and everything to do with guilt, shame, sorrow, apathy, gossip, sex, and normal, devastating unbelief. You will need your comfort kit far more often than your combat gear.

Be a shepherd. The sheep know his voice. They will come to love yours as you speak the Good Shepherd's name.

13

The Temptation to Make
a Name for Myself

Scott Sauls

> And do you seek great things for yourself?
> Seek them not. (Jer. 45:5)

Sometimes the most loving thing God can do is give you your dream job and then take it away.

Dream Come True

The phone call came in 2007. At the time, I was in my fourth year of pastoring and leading a growing, energetic, missional church in St. Louis. As a leader, I felt fulfilled. I met regularly with a couple of local pastors—Darrin and Andrew—who were becoming like brothers, and we were dreaming about how we could bless our city together. I got to teach homiletics (preaching) at Covenant Theological Seminary, which was a joy. Our daughters loved their schools and their friends and were enjoying their childhood. Our friendships were deep and meaningful. Grandma and Grandpa lived two miles away, and we were a half day's drive from the rest of our extended family. Our intentions were to stay in this place, doing this work, together with these people, for the rest of our days.

Then New York City called.

I had been a church planter and pastor for more than a decade. Tim Keller, founding pastor of New York's Redeemer Presbyterian Church, had influenced my preaching, pastoring, and ministerial vision more than everybody else combined. Since seminary, I had carefully studied Tim's teaching, vision, and leadership. Along with this self-directed "distance learning" from a "faculty" of one came a growing attraction to ministry amid the urban core.

Tim had heard about me through Redeemer's executive director, Bruce Terrell. Together, they were searching for a senior leader for the church's vast network of small groups. With the role also came the possibility of entering Redeemer's preaching rotation and, if the leading and preaching went well, becoming an eventual successor to Tim.

After nearly six months of prayer, counseling, and wrestling through the implications of moving our family to New York City, Patti and I accepted the call. In almost no time, we sold virtually everything and moved our family of four into an 850-square-foot, two-bedroom, one-bath apartment on Manhattan's Upper West Side. We fell in love with New York, Redeemer, and the community God had placed around us. The small groups ministry reached record participation, and I was invited into the preaching rotation. After four years of being shaped and groomed for long-term ministry in the city, I was selected to be a lead pastor and one of Tim's four eventual successors.

The first time I heard John Wesley's famous "Covenant Prayer" was at the lead pastor commissioning service:

> I am no longer my own, but yours. Put me to what you will, rank me with whom you will; put me to doing, *put me to suffering*; let me be employed for you, or *laid aside* for you, exalted for you, or

brought low for you; let me be full, *let me be empty,* let me have all things, *let me have nothing:* I freely and wholeheartedly yield all things to your pleasure and disposal. And now, glorious and blessed God, Father, Son and Holy Spirit, you are mine and I am yours. So be it. And the covenant now made on earth, let it be ratified in heaven. Amen.[1]

Then It All Changed

As Wesley's words were prayed that night over the four of us, I did not realize how prophetic the "surrender" parts would be for Patti, our daughters, and me. Within one year, the succession plan changed. For reasons related to timing, sustainability, and strategy, it became clear to the elders that Redeemer would need to adjust its plan for four congregations to three and, therefore, from four lead pastors/successors to three. Nobody had planned for it to work out this way, but sadly, it did. Although Tim and the elders explored several options to ensure that all four of the original lead pastors remained part of Redeemer's future, after much prayer and counsel, one of us ended up resigning—me. It felt like the right thing to do, given the circumstances, but it was devastating. I cried, Patti cried, our children cried, our friends cried.

In retrospect, I can see many reasons why God gave me my dream job in my dream city for a time, only to take it away. One reason is that my current role at Christ Presbyterian Church in Nashville has, in just four years, far exceeded any previous dreaming I had done about other roles in other cities. We are now, more than we could have ever imagined, *home* in Nashville. And in a way, we have been "given back" the dream job—but also much more. Christ Presbyterian, it turns out, was instrumental in sending Tim and Kathy to New York City to start Redeemer three decades ago. And now, having been shaped by Tim's vision more deeply after serving

---

1. From John Wesley, *A Short History of the People Called Methodists,* in *The Complete Works of the Reverend John Wesley, A.M.,* 4th ed., vol. 13 (London: John Mason. 1841), 319, modernized.

alongside him for five years, I am able to bring many of the valuable things I learned in New York to Nashville, which, for all intents and purposes, is becoming the type of city we left.

Even *The New York Times* has referred to Nashville as "The Third Coast," due to its creative, entrepreneurial, culture-making and urbanizing trajectory. Formerly known as a buckle of the Bible Belt, Nashville is swiftly becoming the Athens of the South—a bustling, energetic city whose influence reaches far beyond its own borders. I now understand more fully what Tim said to me in our final breakfast before we left New York: "Scott, we are sad to see you go. But it makes a lot of sense. You are going *to* Nashville *from* Nashville's future."

God's Ambitions Are Better Than Mine

In keeping with Wesley's prayer, the New York experience also brought home the truth that I am not my own but have been bought with a price, and that God's ambitions for my life, whether I understand them or not, are always superior to any I might have for my life. Indeed, it is God's prerogative to do with my life, my family, and my ministry whatever he chooses.

"Put me to what you will . . . let me be employed for you, or laid aside for you."

Thank you, John Wesley. And thank you to the suffering Job and the suffering Jesus. The Lord gives and the Lord takes away; blessed be the name of the Lord (Job 1:21). Lord, "not my will, but yours, be done" (Luke 22:42).

The New York experience also taught me a lot about the nature of ambition, which can be godly and pure, but also self-serving and corrupt. It taught me that I am, on the one hand, a bit like Peter, who, wanting to please his Lord, gladly left everything to follow him (Matt. 19:27–29). On the other hand, I am also a bit like Simon the sorcerer. Remember him? Simon's ambitions, unlike those of Peter and Paul, were self-serving and corrupt. Simon wasn't interested in Jesus using him as a servant for God's glory. Instead, Simon wanted to use Jesus as a servant for Simon's glory:

When Simon saw that the Spirit was given through the laying on of the apostles' hands, he offered them money, saying, "Give me this power also, so that anyone on whom I lay my hands may receive the Holy Spirit." But Peter said to him, "May your silver perish with you, because you thought you could obtain the Gift of God with money! You have no part nor lot in this matter, for your heart is not right before God." (Acts 8:18–21)

I wish it were difficult for me to relate to Simon. Unfortunately, it's not. In some ways, my emotional attachment to New York revealed a similar heart in me, one that in certain ways was *not* right before God.

Just before my resignation, I had an emotional meltdown that lasted for more than three months. I wasn't merely disappointed, which would have been legitimate; I was devastated. I wasn't merely upset, which would have been legitimate; I was crushed. I couldn't sleep at night. I lost my appetite, and with it, between twenty and thirty pounds. I was anxious and depressed. Had I truly been open-handed toward God with *all* of my dreams and hopes and ambitions, had I truly believed the writing of my story belonged to God and not to me, then the thought of walking away from my dream job, though deeply disappointing, would not have wrecked me to the degree it did.

Two Lessons to Learn and Relearn

Looking back, I believe this experience was best not only for Redeemer and Christ Presbyterian but also for Patti, our girls, and me. This has to be true if for no other reason than that it is impossible for God to shortchange any of his children. If we had access to everything God knows and sees about us, then his ways would make perfect sense to us. For me in particular, it was an important wake-up call about two lessons every leader must learn and relearn on a regular basis.

1. Our Failures and Disappointments
Reveal the State of Our Souls

My circumstance-triggered meltdown was at least in part due to idols of success, fame, and making a name for myself that had long lived in my heart. Like hot water through a tea bag, the New York event became the context that exposed ugly ambition in me. Somehow, I had come to believe leading in a global city and pastoring thousands of people with Ivy League degrees, "important" jobs, and household names were the things that would give me significance, justify my existence, and make me esteemed by men. Subconsciously, I related to an anecdote Donald Miller once told about comedian Tom Arnold:

> I caught an interview with Tom Arnold regarding his book *How I Lost Five Pounds in Six Years*. The interviewer asked why he had written the book, and I was somewhat amazed at the honesty of Arnold's answer. The comedian stated that most entertainers are in show business because they are broken people, looking for affirmation. "The reason I wrote this book," Tom Arnold said, "is because I wanted something out there so people would tell me they liked me. It's the reason behind almost everything I do."[2]

Replace "comedian" with "pastor," then replace "show business" with "ministry," and you get the same person with the same issues, only in a different setting and career path. Genuinely good endeavors like comedy and ministry (or the arts, or business, or entrepreneurship, or parenting, or healthcare, or education, or government, or other) become *broken* endeavors when we start depending on them to satisfy our thirst for love, esteem, applause, and approval in ways only Jesus can.

We are famous in God's eyes through Jesus. That should be enough.

Now that we're a few years beyond the New York experience, I hope my heart and ambitions are in a healthier place. I hope my subconscious desire to be the hero of my own story—or any kind of hero for that matter—is fading. I hope my inmost desires are becoming more and more that Jesus would increase and I would decrease—and that I would be deeply satisfied in my role as a supporting actor in *his* story, versus him being a supporting actor in mine. I hope next time my dreams and ambitions are disrupted or grind to a halt—

---

2. Donald Miller, *Searching for God Knows What* (Nashville: Thomas Nelson, 2010), 116.

surely they will be at some point—I will be more prepared to surrender everything to God with an open hand as Job and Jesus did, and to trust deeply the words of a wise old hymn:

Whate'er my God ordains is right:
here shall my stand be taken;
though sorrow, need, or death be mine,
yet I am not forsaken.
My Father's care is round me there;
he holds me that I shall not fall:
and so to him I leave it all.[3]

What might this kind of trust look like in real time? I think it might look like my friend whom I will call Ted, an attorney who got pushed out of his firm not in spite of, but because of, his honest heart.

One day, Ted's supervisor called a private meeting with him. The man told Ted that if he wanted to keep his job, he would have to fudge the truth about a particular client's assets. "If the truth about the client's assets became known by shareholders," the supervisor reasoned, "it would be the end of the client's business and, by extension, the end of a significant income stream coming into the law firm from this client."

Ted, from a place of loyalty to Jesus and a non-negotiable commitment to his integrity, respectfully refused to follow his supervisor's instructions. And he was swiftly terminated from his job. But there was more. It later became clear that Ted's supervisor, by secretly slandering him to potential future employers, blackballed him in virtually every law firm in that city. This resulted in two years of unemployment, which had a deep, painful effect not only on Ted, but also on his wife and three children.

Somewhere in the middle of those two years, I caught Ted before a church service. Jokingly, I asked him if he wanted me to go out and get a jug of gasoline and some matches so we could go set

3. Samuel Rodigast, "Whate'er My God Ordains Is Right," 1675; trans. Catherine Winkworth, 1863; alt. 1961.

his former place of employment on fire, starting with his former supervisor's office. Ted, with a smile and yet a profoundly serious demeanor, looked me straight in the eye and uttered two words I will never forget: "No retribution."

What's on the inside—whatever has *always* been there—will come out when we're squeezed.

How about us? When our dreams and ambitions die, when we lose influence or reputation or a dream job, or when we experience injustice and betrayal like my friend Ted did, what will be revealed about our hearts? Will our hearts show themselves to be "right before God"? As Jesus said, "Will [the Son of Man] find faith on earth?" (Luke 18:8).

2. Our Success and Achievements Are Poor Jesus-Substitutes

C. S. Lewis was onto something when he said: "Aim at heaven and you will get earth thrown in; aim at earth and you will get neither."[4]

I learned this the hard way when, for a season, I allowed ministry in a "notable" city among "notable" people to become an idol. I now see how foolish this thinking was. I see how right Francis Schaeffer was when he said there are *no* little places and *no* little people. If Jesus would choose the small, obscure town of Nazareth as his place of origin and choose to build his kingdom chiefly through people who were *not* wise or powerful or of noble birth (1 Cor. 1:26), how dare I act or think or believe otherwise as I minister in his name.

Recently, I have begun to learn Lewis's and Schaeffer's wisdom in more enjoyable, life-giving ways. Though Nashville and Christ Presbyterian are more similar to New York and Redeemer than different, and though many would look at our current situation and call it a "success story," my perspective on success has changed.

By God's grace, I am thriving in ministry perhaps now more than ever. Since we arrived, God has caused Christ Presbyterian Church

---

4. C. S. Lewis, *Mere Christianity* (San Francisco: Harper, 2001), 134.

to blossom around us. Our staff is unified, and morale is strong. Our elder meetings are forward-thinking, fun, lighthearted, and relational, even as we tend to serious matters of church business. We major in the majors and minor in the minors. Like Redeemer in New York City, our church invests not chiefly in itself but in its city and the world. We focus not on our own preservation but on helping Christians engage thoughtfully with their neighbors and the culture about things that matter. We seek to help them integrate their faith with their work and contribute meaningfully to the elevation of the poor and overlooked and underserved—those living on the margins. I am privileged to pastor and live among and be friends with some of the most lovely, generous, life-giving, and remarkable people I have ever met.

As I think about all these blessings, I am struck by Jesus's admonishment to his disciples precisely when their perceived "success" and "influence" were at their peak:

> The seventy-two returned with joy, saying, "Lord, even the demons are subject to us in your name!" And he said to them, "... Behold, I have given you authority to tread on serpents and scorpions, and over all the power of the enemy, and nothing shall hurt you. Nevertheless, do not rejoice in this, that the spirits are subject to you, but rejoice that your names are written in heaven." (Luke 10:17–20)

When Jesus's disciples brought news of their extraordinary strength and influence and success, his response was, "Do *not* rejoice."

When God gives us success for a time—when he chooses to put the wind at our backs—by all means, we should enjoy it. But we mustn't hang our hats on it, because earthly success, in all its forms, comes to us as a gift from God and is fleeting. Our Lord is telling us not to allow appetizers to replace the feast, or a single apple to replace the orchard, or a road sign to replace the destination to which it points.

On this, Lewis again provides essential wisdom:

It would seem that Our Lord finds our desires not too strong, but too weak. We are half-hearted creatures, fooling about with drink and sex and ambition when infinite joy is offered us, like an ignorant child wants to go on making mud pies in a slum because he cannot imagine what is meant by the offer of a holiday at the sea. We are far too easily pleased.[5]

This perspective reminds us that no self-serving ambition has the ability to satisfy the vastness of the human soul made in God's image. As Augustine aptly said, the Lord has made us for himself. Our hearts will be restless until they find their rest in him.[6]

It is also this perspective from Lewis that is our safeguard from what the famous playwright Tennessee Williams called "The Catastrophe of Success." Williams understood that while things like momentum, influence, position, and being known and celebrated are fine in themselves, none of them can sustain us in the long run. Reflecting on his instant success after the release of his blockbuster Broadway play *The Glass Menagerie*, Williams wrote:

I was snatched out of virtual oblivion and thrust into sudden prominence....

I sat down and looked about me and was suddenly very depressed....

I lived on room service. But in this, too, there was a disenchantment....

I soon found myself becoming indifferent to people. A well of cynicism rose in me....

I got so sick of hearing people say, "I loved your play!" that I could not say thank you any more.... I no longer felt any pride in the play itself but began to dislike it, probably because I felt too lifeless inside ever to create another. I was walking around dead in my shoes....

You know, then, that the public Somebody you are when you "have a name" is a fiction created with mirrors.[7]

---

5. C. S. Lewis, *The Weight of Glory* (New York: HarperOne, 2015), 3.

6. *Confessions* 1.1.1.

7. Tennessee Williams, "The Catastrophe of Success," in *The Glass Menagerie* (New York: New Directions, 1945, 1999), 99–101, 104.

Only Jesus Can Do Helpless Sinners Good

Tennessee Williams's story, as well as that of every person who has experienced the anticlimax of reaching the rainbow's end and finding there is not a pot of gold there after all, confirms a universal truth for every human heart: Only Jesus, whose rule and whose peace shall never cease to increase (Isa. 9:7), can sustain us. Only Jesus, whose resurrection assures us that he is, and forever will be, making all things new, can fulfill our deepest desires and give us a "happily ever after."

Only Jesus can make everything sad come untrue.[8] Only Jesus can ensure a future in which "every chapter is better than the one before."[9]

Only Jesus can give us the glory and the soaring strength of an eagle (Isa. 40:31). Only Jesus, whose name is above every name, and at whose name every knee will bow, can give us a name that will endure forever (Phil. 2:9–10).

Making much of *his* name is, then, a far superior ambition than making a name for ourselves. For apart from Jesus, all men and women, even the most ambitious and successful and strong, will wither away like a vapor.

> The people are grass.
> The grass withers, the flower fades,
>   but the word of our God will stand forever. (Isa. 40:7–8)

If this isn't enough to give us a healthier, humbler perspective on our ambitions, perhaps this observation from Anne Lamott will: "In a hundred years? —All new people."[10]

---

8. To echo J. R. R. Tolkien at the end of *The Return of the King*.
9. To borrow the language of Lewis at the conclusion of *The Last Battle*.
10. Anne Lamott, *All New People: A Novel* (Berkeley, CA: Counterpoint, 1989), 117.

14

The Joy I Can Know
over a Long Tenure

Phil A. Newton

My generation learned a lot about ladders but little about roots.

Talk among my college ministerial association and later seminary community had little to say about putting down roots in a church and staying for the duration. We did ladder talk. Where would we serve to jockey for a larger, more prominent pastorate? How many years would it take to climb the ladder to ministerial success?

I know. Quite carnal.

My friends and I did pulpit supply and youth work but knew little about the staggering realities of pastoral ministry. It was more about preaching than shepherding. I had much to learn. Seminary's academic focus didn't teach me about the joy found in deep roots.

Twenty-five years after those academic days, fifteen years into my present pastorate, someone asked, "How long do you plan on staying at South Woods?" Having not given that question much thought, I blurted, "I guess the rest of my ministry." My mind churned with that hurried comment. Staying for the duration went against youthful naïveté. But by this stage, I found it deeply satisfying. The process since I came to South Woods Baptist Church in Memphis, combined with the horizon ahead, has given me immeasurable joy in the thirty years I've served my congregation. Throughout the time, I've been learning a few lessons about the joy of putting down lasting roots.

The Case for Roots

Accepting a church's call to pastor doesn't guarantee longevity. Some pastors and congregations mesh well. Others don't fit. That might be due to the pastor's lack of maturity, particular gifts, family dynamics, personality, cultural background, or other things. Or it could be due to the congregation's mentality, impatience with the pastor's weaknesses, financial neglect, poor view of the local church, neglect of growth in grace, and other matters. Yet in such a setting where the young pastor has little chance of longevity, he may struggle with guilt over the thought of leaving.

Guilt can freeze a young pastor into ministerial idealism. But guilt doesn't cultivate joy. It stymies pastoral roots and offers a poor rationale for a long tenure. One young man expressed such guilt to me; I nudged him to consider another ministry where he might better use his gifts. His move has proven fruitful as his roots have kept digging deeper.

That doesn't mean moving is always best. A healthy pause to survey the field of ministry may slow down "greener pasture syndrome." Short pastorates may pay scant attention to the potential of sustained ministry that endures seasons and strains that ultimately lead to joy.

We went through such a season around years six to eight in my pastorate. Sundays were difficult. Murmuring and dissension challenged my focus. But the Lord sustained me in the time of strife and weakness. There were things I needed to learn about grace, perseverance, pastoral ministry, and true joy that could only be discovered in the fire.

People left, finances dipped, but the gift of unity in the body grew unexpectedly. I would have missed the unbridled joy of unity in Christ that the fire refines and polishes, had I peered too long over the fence and bolted to another pasture. Some joys can be experienced only in the grace of perseverance.

Overcoming Guilt of Pulling Up Roots

We're not all like eighteenth-century English pastor Robert Hall Sr., who weathered six years of bitter opposition by a few power mongers and then spent the rest of his life—thirty-eight years—serving one church. Some of us identify with his contemporary Andrew Fuller, who after a few years serving the church at Soham, England, struggled with the continued inquiries of the Kettering church. He feared pride would be his motive in moving to a larger congregation.

Hall counseled him to consider the invitation to Kettering. Fuller balked and waited for another year before accepting their call. His friend John Ryland Jr. remarked, "Men who fear not God would risk the welfare of a nation with fewer searchings of heart than it cost him to determine whether he should leave a little dissenting church, scarcely containing forty members besides himself and his wife."[1]

After eight years in Soham, Fuller served the Kettering church for thirty-three years and, under his leadership, profoundly affected evangelical work in Britain and the early missionary movement. But Fuller had to get over the guilt of leaving before he could put down roots in Kettering. That didn't make the Kettering ministry easy. Rather, the soil of Soham did not accommodate roots best suited for Kettering.

Bumps in the Journey

Whether for Hall or Fuller, you or me, pastoral longevity meets with bumps along the journey. The seminarian's dream of smooth pastoral sailing is a mirage. Shepherding involves dealing with sheep. Sheep are messy. And the shepherd is not the sweetest-smelling

---

1. Andrew Gunton Fuller, *Andrew Fuller* (London: Hodder and Stoughton, 1882), 50.

fellow on the hillside either. The clash of personalities, spiritual warfare, unregenerate church members, turf lords, power grabbing, communication failures, misunderstandings, leadership changes, expositional preaching, theological clarity, immaturity, and inexperience all combine to create bumps—sometimes big bumps. However, that's the pastoral journey.

If a pastor does more than the typical three- or four-year stopover on the way to bigger and better things, he will need to learn to persevere through the bumps.

Only in a ministry that presses on through difficulties will a pastor know the joys of triumph in spiritual warfare, the unity of once-conflicting personalities, and the reordering of polity structures to practice servant leadership. On two occasions, six to eight years after removing members through church discipline, I experienced the joy of asking our congregation to restore them to fellowship. A *journeyman* pastor would likely have missed out on that total picture of redemptive church discipline work.

Do My Roots Fit This Soil?

Realistically, the soil of a particular church may not fit well the roots of a pastor. Yet he must test the soil by being faithful in life, satisfied in Christ, humble in shepherding, and dogged in perseverance. It may take a few years to see whether or not the Lord has planted him in a church for the long term.

What does it take for this kind of endurance? At least four things:

1. Passion for the Congregation

A pastor can look at his duties as a mere means of compensation until something better comes along. However, the Lord of the church calls us to humbly shepherd and serve a portion of his flock, feeding them the Word, comforting them in need, correcting the erring, encouraging perseverance, and exemplifying faithfulness to Christ (Acts 20:28; 1 Tim. 4:11–16; 6:17–21; 2 Tim. 2:1–26; 3:10–4:5; Heb. 13:17; 1 Pet. 5:1–4). The fruit in that kind of ministry may be long in coming, but it's certain when the pastor stays with the flock.

I once tried to talk a brother out of accepting a church's pastoral call. The problem was not the church but that brother. He viewed the pastorate as a preaching station. He wanted to preach but scarcely noticed the sheep. His short tenure ended unhappily. He had no passion for them.

Passion for the flock grows when we spend time with them, listen to them, serve them, and pray for them. I didn't grasp that well in my early pastorates. I liked serving them and enjoyed spending time with *some* of them, but regularly praying for and listening to them didn't quite fit my busy routine. I had years to go before I developed the passion for a congregation with whom I might spend my entire ministry.

2. *Willingness to Persevere*

Perseverance taxes us. Without perseverance, a discouragement like a testy elders meeting, a disagreement with staff, a run-in with an ornery member, or being the brunt of a rumor leads to updating the résumé. Long pastorates are always tested pastorates. Perseverance becomes the grace-laden tracks on which long pastorates run to the finish line.

Charles Spurgeon could easily have quit or moved to a less demanding ministry after the Surrey Garden disaster of 1856 that almost cost him health and sanity. Opponents created a stir, causing a stampede from the crowded music hall that left seven dead and twenty-eight seriously injured. Few would have blamed Spurgeon for leaving. But by the grace of God he persevered. Recovering from the strain, he ministered with growing influence. He mused, "What a fool the devil is! If he had not vilified me, I should not have had so many precious souls as my hearers."[2] He saw fruitful ministry by persevering through adversities.

---

2. Charles Haddon Spurgeon, *Letters of C. H. Spurgeon*, ed. Iain Murray (Edinburgh: Banner of Truth, 1991), 56–57, cited in Tom Nettles, *Living by Revealed Truth: The Life and Pastoral Theology of Charles Haddon Spurgeon* (Fearn, Ross-shire, UK: Mentor, 2013), 93.

3. Discipline for the Long Haul

Long tenures require developing sustainable patterns for study, counseling, leadership development, prayer, administration, and communication. A pastor can't just let these things happen. Administration, for instance, may so sap a pastor's mental energies, he has nothing left for sermon preparation.

In early years, I often jumped from one thing to another in harried attempts to accomplish everything I thought people expected of me. My drained mind grew frustrated with doing a hundred different things and left me staring blankly at Sunday's text.

Learn to set boundaries on your schedule. You cannot do everything, so conquer the Superman complex. Be willing to delegate to others while you give attention to what you do best. Sometimes you'll still need to dirty your hands with a clogged toilet or some other mundane issue. You're a servant, so be willing to serve. But you're also a servant ministering the Word and shepherding the flock, so prioritize your schedule while doing so with grace and gentleness toward others (Acts 6).

Beware of burning out by not scheduling time off. You can't persevere long without an occasional pause in your routine. After the excited disciples returned from ministry, Jesus took them aside to rest (Matt. 9:10). As Vance Havner once quipped, "If you don't come apart, you will come apart!"[3] Christopher Ash counsels us, "There is a difference between godly sacrifice and needless burnout."[4] We must learn the difference to maintain our pace in the long journey.

4. Develop Lay and Staff Elders (Leaders)

You are not a one-man show. If that's your desire, join a circus and stay out of ministry. You're *the leader* of the team serving a congregation. Study Paul's ministry. He exceeded the average person's abilities, yet he worked with a team around him. He trained others

---

3. Vance Havner, *Pepper 'n Salt* (Westwood, NJ: Revell, 1966), http://vancehavner.com/?s=you+will+come+apart.

4. Christopher Ash, *Zeal without Burnout: Seven Keys to a Lifelong Ministry of Sustainable Sacrifice* (London: Good Book, 2016), 40–41.

to serve with him and in the churches that he planted (in *The Mentoring Church*, I trace his training process).[5]

As Paul told Timothy, "What you have heard from me in the presence of many witnesses entrust to faithful men, who will be able to teach others also" (2 Tim. 2:2). Timothy was evidence that Paul did what he had told Timothy to do. You cannot sustain the demands of a lengthy ministry with healthy mind and heart apart from developing leaders around you who join in the work. Plus, you cannot develop the next generation of spiritual leaders by hopping from one church to another. One of my greatest joys has been the *slow process* of training future elders, pastors, missionaries, and leaders. In a short pastorate, that wouldn't have happened.

Relationships Make for Longevity

I was too young when I was ordained but had enough sense to reject one deeply flawed piece of advice. A neighboring pastor told me, "Don't get too close to your people." Alarms went off. Amazingly, I kept my mouth shut at such blatantly bad counsel. You won't shepherd those you're unwilling to get close to. You certainly won't persevere in pastoral ministry if you keep the congregation at arm's length. You need close relationships that endure the years to help shape you too.

How? Here are six lines of advice:

1. *Invest.* A fellow elder and I were riding with a missionary in his community when he told us he needed to stop at a house and *invest* in someone. We wondered what he meant. As we thought about that financial term, we realized it fittingly described pastoral relationships. You invest what is valuable to you to expand its value. As pastors we invest time, thought, energy, love, and service in those we desire to see living in faithfulness to Christ. Long tenures allow you the joy of seeing returns on your *investment.*

2. *Pray.* As a young pastor, I heard another pastor say he prayed each week for every member of his church. At that point, I was much

5. Phil A. Newton, *The Mentoring Church: How Pastors and Congregations Cultivate Leaders* (Grand Rapids, MI: Kregel, 2017).

too lazy in my prayer life for such a discipline—even with my much smaller congregation. His comment rebuked me. It changed my pastoral relationships. You will build long relationships with those you regularly take before the throne of grace. As you labor in prayer for them, you grow in love, passion, and longing for the flock. You find that despite their many idiosyncrasies, you want to stay with them. Calling them *family* is no longer ministerial bravado. The years prove that you gladly feel it.

3. *Listen.* The idea of relationships involves communication. The largest side of communication is listening. As those accustomed to speaking, we sometimes struggle to sit and listen. We want to dish out our nicely framed speech and then hurry to the next thing on our list. But relationships call for patience, gentleness, and tenderness. When you spend time listening, you find satisfaction in serving a brother or sister. In the process, your roots dig deeper into the congregation's soil.

4. *Get involved.* Involve yourself in the joys and sorrows of your congregation. As the pastor you will likely be called on if there's a death or tragedy. Be there with heart and soul. Join in knowing and rejoicing in your members' joys too.

After thirty years with the same congregation, I've listened to problems, rejoiced at successes, shared burdens, wept at losses, and laughed at joys. That builds relationships that endure difficult days and makes room for others to accept my faults and weaknesses.

5. *Shepherd.* Shepherd the flock rather than preaching *at* them. Think of the congregation as you prepare to stand before them to open the Word. Pray through your sermon with them on your heart. Look at them while you preach. Envision their heart cries, burdens, and needs as you apply the Word. The Lord of the church entrusted the flock, with all of its faults, to you. So let the roots dig deep into their lives. The long journey with them enriches your preaching with tender compassion, careful application, and confident hope in Christ. Your preaching will become more transparent as you, with all of your weaknesses, trust in Christ to shepherd your flock.

6. *Cherish.* Cherish the diversity of the church as it displays the

beauty and power of the gospel. If everyone were like you or me, the congregation would be entirely boring. Think often and pray more with gratitude that the Lord has put different backgrounds, ethnicities, personalities, and interests into the flock that you're called to serve. Instead of complaining about their tics, give thanks that Christ is pleased to show forth his glory among such a people and that he finds pleasure in your serving them. The pastoral transformation that results from cherishing the flock leaves you with untold joy in your calling.

Strong Roots

Ladders work well for climbing immoveable structures, but they lose their passengers when winds blow and structures shake. Strong roots, however, withstand the wind and storms, remaining firm and steadfast.

Pastoral ministry traffics in the storms. Only with strong roots in the congregation can pastors, by God's grace, experience the immeasurable joy found in long ministry with a people.

15

What to Do When No Church Hires Me

Collin Hansen

I never wanted this job. When I resigned from a job I loved as news editor of *Christianity Today* to enroll in seminary, I fully expected to assume a pastoral position three years later. I even accepted a generous scholarship that demanded I find work as a pastor immediately upon graduation. I wanted to preach. To counsel. To disciple new believers. To mourn and pray with people in their most difficult moments. To set a vision for local church ministry that would make much of Jesus.

But I couldn't get hired. By anyone. And not for lack of trying! Only God knows the reasons why. That doesn't stop me from speculating, though.

My job search came in the aftermath of the Great Recession. With their savings decimated, older pastors weren't retiring, which meant younger pastors weren't moving up, which meant even younger pastors weren't moving in. Maybe, then, I just had bad timing. My fellow graduates didn't fare much better in that market.

I also found the job-search process for churches just plain weird and confusing. I was open to various possibilities: solo pastor in a small church, associate pastor in a large church, even church planting in the right scenario.

Let me share an incomplete list of job leads gone cold.

One denominational leader asked if I would be willing to move to northern Minnesota. The offer sounded fine to this South Dakota farm boy, as I temporarily forgot that I had married a woman from Alabama. I asked for more information. Turns out the church had an opening because the pastor split from his elders to start a new congregation on the other side of this same small town. Didn't sound "Minnesota nice" to me.

I searched closer to my wife's hometown. I reached out to one of only two churches in Alabama from my denomination. The senior pastor said, "Yes, we have an opening, because our associate pastor is leaving to plant a new church in another city." He asked for my résumé. I sent it. I never heard back. I looked up the associate pastor and found that his theology didn't at all fit our denomination's. No wonder we didn't match.

Within the same denomination, I talked to a church in a large college town. The chair of the search committee told me he might be interested in the job himself. He just hadn't yet decided whether or not to toss his name into the hat. No thanks.

Yet another denominational leader told me I was a good candidate for church planting. He recommended a Big Ten college town in the Midwest. I asked which one. He mentioned Bloomington. And Iowa City. And West Lafayette. And so on. I'm not even a church-planting expert, but I can name every town in the Big Ten. And, of course, there was no money to support me.

In yet another college town, I asked a part-time pastor if he needed an assistant. Instead, he suggested I consider planting a church across the street. I still don't know if I was intended to take that advice as a compliment or an insult.

At this point you're probably wondering what's wrong with me. Me too. At one large church where I had many connections, the executive pastor said he would fly to my city to do the interview. My wife visited friends in that town to see what she thought of the place. No bother, because I never heard from him again. In a similar situation one entry-level pastor had been dispatched to interview seminarians. He couldn't understand why I wanted the job as he looked over my résumé with a mixture of church and journalism experience. So I told him how God had called me to be a pastor. I guess he didn't buy it.

Then there was the usual mixture of ordinary rejections. One church never bothered to take down their job listing after they filled it. Another church seemed really interested, but they just went in a different direction. My own church found a better-qualified candidate for their only open position. Just a few weeks into my current job I told one senior pastor that I had applied for a low-level position at his church and had never heard back. He was incredulous! They would've strongly considered me, he said.

It wasn't to be.

It probably took longer than necessary for me to take the hint. For whatever reason, God didn't want me to be a pastor. At least not now. After my failed search I met with my old boss, who kindly offered me a new job and a 50 percent pay increase. I recited my litany of rejections, and he said something I'll never forget: "You know, Collin, a subjective call is one thing. But it doesn't mean anything without an objective call."

And that's what seminary didn't teach me.

Two Conclusions

Seminary will test any man's sense of calling. I don't mean in admissions. There's always a seminary that will take you. I mean the grueling mixture of spiritual turmoil with graduate-level academics. If Greek doesn't get you, then Hebrew probably will. Somewhere around the third church history course many students wonder how many more heresies they can be expected to recall on demand—and how any of it is supposed to help in ministry. The practical theology courses on preaching and counseling and leadership can be beneficial, but no one pretends that case studies alone can substitute for learning by trial and error. In pastoral ministry the trials are sure to come, and the errors won't be long in following.

The test of my calling came not in any of these classes but in that moment with my former boss. Could I really be called as a pastor if no church called me to be *their* pastor? How was I supposed to read the circumstances? Was God saying "not now" or "never"? With the Spirit's help I resolved the dilemma with two conclusions:

1. *I have much more room to grow in the character qualifications for ministry.* Well before I left my job, and then as a church intern and seminary student, I studied the biblical lists of qualifications for overseers. The list in 1 Timothy 3:1–7 is the most extensive:

> The saying is trustworthy: If anyone aspires to the office of overseer, he desires a noble task. Therefore an overseer must be above reproach, the husband of one wife, sober-minded, self-controlled, respectable, hospitable, able to teach, not a drunkard, not violent but gentle, not quarrelsome, not a lover of money. He must manage his own household well, with all dignity keeping his children submissive, for if someone does not know how to manage his own household, how will he care for God's church? He must not be a recent convert, or he may become puffed up with conceit and fall into the condemnation of the devil. Moreover, he must be well thought of by outsiders, so that he may not fall into disgrace, into a snare of the devil.

No one who taught, mentored, or interviewed me suggested I might be disqualified from ministry for one of these reasons. Nevertheless, no one knew my heart as well as I did. Was I really ready to serve the body of Christ as a pastor? In retrospect, probably not. To cite just a few examples, I wouldn't have regarded myself as particularly hospitable, gentle, peaceable, or self-controlled. If anything, God worked through the disappointment and failure of my job search to reveal these sins.

In some ways my life fell apart when I couldn't get hired as a pastor out of seminary. My wife and I lost nearly $100,000 in the housing crisis. Though we tried for several years, she could not get pregnant. These strains took a severe toll on our marriage. I struggled to pastor my own household well. How could I presume to lead a church?

Eight years later I can see how the Lord worked in these circumstances to grow me in Christlikeness. He used the disappointment to lead me to the end of myself. So long as I boasted in my résumé and wondered why no one would hire me, I could not truly minister in the power of God. The apostle Paul's words in 1 Corinthians 1:26–31 ring true now in ways I couldn't hear back then:

> For consider your calling, brothers: not many of you were wise according to worldly standards, not many were powerful, not many were of noble birth. But God chose what is foolish in the world to shame the wise; God chose what is weak in the world to shame the strong; God chose what is low and despised in the world, even things that are not, to bring to nothing things that are, so that no human being might boast in the presence of God. And because of him you are in Christ Jesus, who became to us wisdom from God, righteousness and sanctification and redemption, so that, as it is written, "Let the one who boasts, boast in the Lord."

Is any man ever ready for that kind of Pauline ministry? It's like asking if someone is really ready for marriage. Some things you just need to learn the hard way. I learned, after I couldn't get hired, just how much more room I needed to grow in the most important qualifications for ministry.

2. Before I am called to any position, I'm gifted by God to serve. The job search for pastors usually looks quite a bit different from the way we identify elders. And I wonder if that's often a mistake. When we're looking for lay elders, we understand that a man won't suddenly start acting like an elder when he's appointed to the office. Rather, we look for a man already doing the job. He welcomes people into his home. He leads his family with deliberate spiritual intent. He works in a way his peers publicly commend. He gives generously.

He seeks peace. He studies and teaches the Bible to build up the body of Christ. And so on. Your church hopefully has many such elders-in-all-but-title.

I don't blame the churches that didn't hire me as their pastor. What could they really know about me from a sheet of paper? Still, without an external call from one of these churches, I had to ask myself, *Am I actually meant to serve at all as a church leader?*

God was kind to reveal an answer: my gifting for service doesn't change just because I'm paid to do it. If I'm a teacher, I'll teach. I might not be preaching from the pulpit every week, but there are always new and young believers looking to learn. I'm not paid to set the church's agenda, but I can still pray for the pastors and offer my support and even my counsel when they request it. I can always make my home a welcoming place for unbelievers to learn about Jesus and see him work in power.

This perspective on gifting and calling freed me to join a congregation and serve without regard for title, position, and pay. I never lacked for opportunity, because the church never lacks for need. I served four years in various capacities—small group leader, fill-in preacher, spiritual mentor, and more—before the church called me as an elder. In this role I'm doing just about everything I ever expected to as a pastor, except for preaching. And who knows, perhaps that call will come someday as well. I'm content to wait on the Lord's timing.

Make a Man a Minister

Once I took this job I never wanted, pastoral positions suddenly opened. One church that earlier seemed ambivalent toward me warmed after they received a couple of strong recommendations. A friend at my own church moved on and inquired about my interest in replacing him in a highly desired role. But by that time I'd accepted my current job at the Gospel Coalition, and I couldn't leave my new colleagues in the lurch. I'm glad I didn't, but I'll always wonder what might have been.

In this life I'll probably never understand everything God has been doing in this process, especially if I never become a pastor, as I still desire.

Seminary did teach me a great deal—how to interpret the Bible using original languages, how to put together the Old and New Testaments, how to prepare a sermon, how to avoid the mistakes of church history, and much more. I wouldn't trade my seminary experience for anything. Even today I work out of a seminary office and invest much of my time in training prospective young ministers. Seminaries are valuable, even necessary, for the health of today's church.

But seminary didn't teach me what to do when I couldn't get hired. It didn't prepare me to navigate a confusing job search or show me what to do when I needed to get a job and provide for my family. And I don't know how it could have. I would have been unwise to expect as much.

Throughout this book, from the perspective of various writers, you've seen that seminary is valuable but not sufficient. We do not intend to denigrate the valuable work of seminaries. Rather, we want to help young pastors, seminary students, and other aspiring ministers learn from our experience how God fits a man to be a faithful and effective minister.

The local church won't soon displace what only seminaries can teach us. But only the local church under the authority of God can make a man a minister.

Contributors

Daniel L. Akin is president of Southeastern Baptist Theological Seminary in Wake Forest, North Carolina, and is a council member with the Gospel Coalition.

Matt Capps is senior pastor of Fairview Baptist Church in Apex, North Carolina.

Collin Hansen is editorial director for the Gospel Coalition and serves on the advisory board of Beeson Divinity School.

Jeff Higbie is pastor of Faith Evangelical Church in Underwood, North Dakota.

Matt McCullough is pastor of Trinity Church in Nashville, Tennessee.

Phil A. Newton is senior pastor of South Woods Baptist Church in Memphis, Tennessee.

John Onwuchekwa is pastor of Cornerstone Church in Atlanta, Georgia.

Vermon Pierre is lead pastor at Roosevelt Community Church in Phoenix, Arizona.

Harry L. Reeder is senior pastor of Briarwood Presbyterian Church (PCA) in Birmingham, Alabama, and a council member with the Gospel Coalition.

Jeff Robinson Sr. is senior editor for the Gospel Coalition and pastor of Christ Fellowship Church in Louisville, Kentucky.

Juan Sanchez is senior pastor of High Pointe Baptist Church in Austin, Texas, and a council member with the Gospel Coalition.

Scott Sauls is senior minister at Christ Presbyterian Church (PCA) in Nashville, Tennessee.

Jay Thomas is pastor of Chapel Hill Bible Church in Chapel Hill, North Carolina.

Dale Van Dyke is pastor of Harvest Church (OPC) in Wyoming, Michigan.

Mark Vroegop is lead pastor of College Park Church in Indianapolis, Indiana.

General Index

Scripture Index

Also Available from
The Gospel Coalition

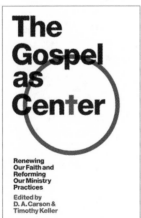

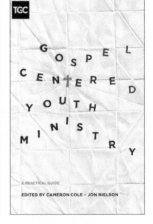

For more information, visit crossway.org.

THE GOSPEL **COALITION**

The Gospel Coalition is a fellowship of evangelical churches deeply committed to renewing our faith in the gospel of Christ and to reforming our ministry practices to conform fully to the Scriptures. We have committed ourselves to invigorating churches with new hope and compelling joy based on the promises received by grace alone through faith alone in Christ alone.

We desire to champion the gospel with clarity, compassion, courage, and joy—gladly linking hearts with fellow believers across denominational, ethnic, and class lines. We yearn to work with all who, in addition to embracing our confession and theological vision for ministry, seek the lordship of Christ over the whole of life with unabashed hope in the power of the Holy Spirit to transform individuals, communities, and cultures.

Through its pastoral resources, The Gospel Coalition aims to encourage and equip current and prospective pastors for faithful endurance over a lifetime of ministry in the church. By learning from experienced ministers of different ages, races, and nationalities, we hope to grow together in godly maturity as the Spirit leads us in the way of Jesus Christ.

Join the cause and visit TGC.org for fresh resources that will equip you to love God with all your heart, soul, mind, and strength, and to love your neighbor as yourself.

TGC.org